Teaching Creative Drama

BRENDA WALKER

Teaching Creative Drama

Age group 9 to 15 years

B T Batsford Limited

First published 1970
Reprinted 1971
7134 2068 5

Reproduced and Printed in Great Britain by
Redwood Press Limited, Trowbridge & London
Bound by Hunter & Foulis, Edinburgh
for the publishers
B T Batsford Limited, 4 Fitzhardinge Street, London W1

Contents

Contents   7

Acknowledgment

I would like to thank Mr A. W. Rowe, BA MPhil, LRAM, Headmaster of the David Lister High School Kingston upon Hull for an exciting and stimulating period of teaching and also for giving permission to use extracts from the programme of *Land of Golden Days*. This was written by Mr Raymond White, Head of the English Department. The comments on *The Gun* were written by Mr Anthony Halford, also on the English staff at that time. The pupils of this school were largely responsible for the creative ideas illustrated in the sample lessons. I would like to thank them and also other members of staff who took an active interest in the work.

I am particularly grateful to Mr W. W. Wynne, Vice-Principal of Endsleigh College of Education and to Mr S. C. Evernden, Head of Drama, Loughborough College of Education for their encouragement and constructive help.

I am pleased to acknowledge permission to reproduce extracts of copyright material from the following: J. M. Dent and Sons Ltd for *Doctor and the Devils* and *Under Milk Wood* by Dylan Thomas; Albert Bonniers Forlag for *The Wonderful Adventure of Nils* by Victor Petterson; Robin Pemberton-Billing, Director of the Octagon Theatre, Bolton for the adaptation of *Doctor and the Devils* by Dylan Thomas, the Literary Trustees of Walter de la Mare for his poem *Drugged;* Margery Vosper Ltd for *Goodbye To All That* by Robert Graves published by Cassell and Co Ltd; Curtis Brown Ltd for *Journey's End* by R. C. Sheriff published by Samuel French; the Hamlyn Publishing Group Ltd for *The Churchill Anthology* by Winston S. Churchill; Michael Joseph Ltd for *The Day of Glory* by H. E. Bates; G. T. Sassoon for the newspaper account and poem by Siegfried Sassoon; Mr Harold Owen and Chatto and Windus Ltd for the poems of Wilfrid Owen; and the Rev C. Ian Pettitt, Vicar of Chingford for the extract from his Parish Magazine.

The text of the Authorised Version of the Bible is Crown Copyright and the extracts used herein are reproduced by permission of Eyre and Spottiswoode Ltd.

Chingford 1970   B W

Introduction

A VARIETY OF APPROACHES TO CREATIVE DRAMA

This book is designed for the teacher who has a little experience of creative drama, who realises that there is great value in such work and would like some guidance in how to set about it with a sense of progression.

It is natural that any approach to such a wide subject should be a personal one; teachers with different interests will feel secure approaching the lesson from their own particular subject. This may be History, English Literature, Religion, Geography, Poetry or Art, but it would be a pity to withhold such a dimension of related experience merely because the class teacher has no personal knowledge of Educational Drama. I refer here not only to theoretical but to practical experience. Very often local drama associations or colleges, hold sessions where the non-specialist can try for himself the tripartite aspect of music, movement, and improvisation. If the thought of movement is inhibiting it is worth experimenting with improvisation alone, for only by 'doing' can the situation really be explored and the child's early reactions to the work appreciated.

Drama is really synonymous with play, whatever its definition, and we all need, even as adults, an opportunity to express this inborn instinct. It is also a form of 'sympathetic magic'. The child talks to himself taking the identity of many characters; the adult mentally rearranges the conversation which has just taken place in an attempt to resolve an outcome favourable to himself. The 9 to 15 age group have not the opportunities of the infant play corner or imaginative playground and it will be left to the conscience of the teacher to provide such opportunities within any appropriate lesson. If the teacher opts out, the children's need for imaginative play could well lead them, unobserved, into the realm of theft, wilful damage and gang warfare.

To many people the concept of the drama lesson is still a formal one. They imagine the young child reading badly, acting in front of the class with the end product in mind being the school play. To others, however, there is the suggestion of the use of music, movement and improvisation, but no clear idea of why they should be included. As we consider the value of this work and our specific aim in each lesson, it should become clear that we are trying to develop children as people, and the fact that they may become first rate actors is of secondary importance.

Take for example a group or class working on an improvisation. They are learning to select and shape their own ideas. It is an exercise not only in verbal but in emotional communication. There is an opportunity for decision making. The natural leaders emerge and the children discover a sensitive awareness of the needs of others. Children who have difficulty in making friends, or those who demand a great deal of personal attention, discover that co-operation and the sharing of ideas can be a creative and satisfying occupation. They identify with a role and perhaps in the process make a discovery about human nature.

Another example is a class of children responding individually to music, teacher's narration, or the two simultaneously. They are not only being stimulated imaginatively, but they are developing their powers of concentration and self-control. They may have been stimulated by a painting, colour slide or film. Then they would have been exercising the gift of sight, observing in large dimension or fine detail; seeing beyond the obvious. They may have been stimulated by sound, thus learning to listen and distinguish different levels of sound.

A baby develops a sense of touch through exploration and close contact with its mother. It will stroke its mother's skin while feeding, later transferring this to a blanket or pillow-slip. As the child grows he is forbidden to touch and yet he learns by touch. The class which discusses touch, its means of communication and its taboos will understand their reactions, not only in the acted scene but in real life. Smell should not be omitted but treated in a similar manner. Such an awareness of the senses is a fulfilment of one aspect of their personalities.

When the class works in a similar manner but with small

groups, it is possible for them to achieve an aesthetic pleasure in creating a work of art in human sculpture through an awareness of space, level, pattern and rhythm. They are imagining contrasting levels of experience which could stimulate oral expression. Involvement of the spoken word in poetry or prose enables the child to discover the music within his own voice.

It has been said that little good creative work appears where the relationships between child and child, and child and teacher are not themselves conducive to understanding and mutual respect. For drama to succeed in the lesson, the teacher must have a good relationship with the class, with a firm but pleasant control which transfers easily from the classroom to the large hall. If this relationship is well established the drama should very soon have a sincere approach. This sincerity grows with the absorption and self-control of the group. This in turn grows with the confidence of the teacher, the clarity of his instruction and the quality of leadership he shows as a member of the group.

Drama is self-generating in ideas; it is an exploration of human relationships; a shared experience of creation or of the beauty, joys and sorrows of life; it is a vital part of literature, music and art.

SOUND

The stimulus of music adds another dimension to the drama lesson. It can capture the imagination, or set the mood for dialogue or occupational activities. However, if it is mis-used it will do none of these things. The music should be carefully chosen, matching the musical intensity with the activity. Records are an expensive item, but often jumble sales or secondhand shops reveal excellent quality 78s for a few pence. A music list is included which may help with selection (page 138). Where limited money is available, the records marked with an asterisk give a reasonable quantity of contrasting material.

Music, whether on tape or record, needs to be handled sensitively during the lesson. Too long a pause while finding the place, the jarring of the needle, sudden volume or quick fade, will break any atmosphere of concentration there may have been.

Any sound can be used as a control. Where a record is used, the class should be quiet, ready to listen for the first notes. If they are to stop suddenly, the record should be faded quickly; if the activity is to cease slowly and then stop completely, a gentle fade and complete silence for a second or two will help achieve this. A game, such as musical statues, helps to build in this particular response.

Percussion instruments can be equally effective. An instrument such as a drum can be used as a signal to control a class when they are doing work which involves excited improvisation. This creates a short sharp sound easily distinguished over excited voices or the clatter of rostra being moved. The cymbal gives a continuing sound and often accompanies a similar quality of movement. It can either set or end a scene.

Glockenspiel, recorder, sleigh bells, castanets, Chinese skulls, triangle and tambourine can all stimulate the imagination or accompany movement. Home made sounds are more challenging for creation and the children will delight in their construction.

The human voice is also a musical instrument. If records are not available then the teacher has to rely on voice alone. The teacher should be able to set the mood or describe the scene not just in words which are black and white, but in words which convey colour and feeling.

> *eg* The grey mist swirled about them and it was quiet... they were conscious of their hearts beating...they continued peering into the darkness listening...suddenly...there was a sound behind them. They leaped back, flailing the air with their swords...but there was nothing, nothing but the mist.

Through these words should come the dampness and the dark, the anticipation and the fear, the tense concentration, the listening and the waiting. Then the sudden rush of adrenalin, the defence against attack, the panic; the sudden realisation of renewed fear.

Technically, this is done from the presence of these thoughts in the mind of the narrator so that he is, in fact, living the sequence. In this way the timing will be correct for the length of pause before the sudden turn, by allowing the words which have a sound sense, such as *mist, swirled, fear, flailing, darkness* and *dampness,* an extension of their continuing sounds or a sharpness of the shorter ones. Some words have a quality of movement or stillness, *eg listening, peering flailing.* The vocal pitch sets the mood. In the example the pitch changes on the word *suddenly* and returns to its original pitch on *but there was nothing, nothing but the mist.* The speed of delivery is important. The slowness of the search and its continuation at the end of the passage contrasts with the sudden spurt in the centre.

At the end of improvising to such a narration the class are imaginatively involved and any further direction following this should come in a quiet tone not unlike the end of the passage. In this way the shock of jerking them too harshly back to reality is avoided. Every lesson should have some form of de-climax whether it be built into the story, takes the form of discussion or is just listening to music.

AUDIENCE

When a piece of creative work is polished and shown to an audience it takes on a different quality. Sometimes this is to advantage with a certain amount of creative work still going on within its framework. For some inexperienced groups ' showing ' to others creates artificiality. There is the sincere comic line which receives sincere laughter from the audience. The child is tempted now to play for laughs. It is no longer an exploration of a situation but a piece of theatre and to be good it demands the techniques of a good actor. ' Speak up please; We can't see you ', are tempting remarks in this situation.

The sensitive teacher is well aware of the child who needs to show his work to others. Very often it is the one with the reputation handed on from year to year, a role he lives up to; or the eager child, verbose and gregarious. For that child showing may be an important part of the development of his personality. Only the teacher concerned really knows when the time is ripe. If all the class were to show each other irrespective of need, it may create an air of competition which is not always desirable in the drama lesson. It could defeat all that was being attempted in securing the confidence of the class. To say a group is good implies there was a bad. If a class votes for the best, or worse still, which ' actor ' was the best, or if adverse criticism of group or individual suggestions is given, ideas will run out because the class will soon stop contributing.

Compare it to learning any other skill. You practise to perfect it. You do not want to show it before you have reached this stage and risk having it criticised. You may share the experience with your personal friends or someone you trust because their encouragement gives you self-confidence to go on and reach perhaps not perfection in the eyes of the world but something which is satisfaction for you.

MOVEMENT

When we speak of movement we think of dance. Sometimes in drama movement does develop into dance. It may begin with some simple activity which, when it takes on an emotional content, flows with the music and although it may lack qualities of movement technique, it is certainly a personal style of dance...a personal interpretation of sound using the mind and body with sincerity and absorption.

Sound is very much part of life and it is difficult to omit this from an improvisation. With sound comes atmosphere and the body responds to both; that it why it is difficult to use music without involving 'movement'.

The lesson that is entirely devoted to drama may often start with what is called a 'warm-up session'. The aim perhaps being to get the class moving physically and rid them of excess energy. There should, however, be some relation to the work that follows if the session is to have any other lasting value. A certain amount of unconnected work may be necessary when experimenting with the control factor, but afterwards very little imagination is needed to adapt ideas and link them in theme with the work that follows.

DANCE DRAMA

I do not suggest that the child's attention is drawn to any specific part of the body at any one time, *eg* exercises for feet, hands, etc, because I feel that if the child's imagination is captured, the child will express in his own personal way how his feet would move in sand or water. It may need a little suggestion on the part of the teacher, but to separate it into exercises where the concentration is on 'what should I be doing with my feet?' rather than 'the water is cold and I find it difficult to walk' seems artificial, demanding a mass rather than a personal approach to expression.

I feel the quality of the movement should be approached through the imagination or in a separate dance lesson. Girls who learn Modern Educational Dance are learning to use their bodies as an instrument of expression. They learn a movement vocabulary and then interpret this vocabulary in a personal way, thus bringing to the drama lesson another dimension. It is only when this vocabulary is not personalised, and the child is more concerned with the movement than with imagination, that Modern Educational Dance tends to be criticised by those connected with Drama in Education. Aesthetic or artistic qualities of grouping which includes motivation and emphasis, should be discussed and with this comes the relationship of one person's movement with another, and the observation of the body's natural position in joy, grief, etc, so that they can be extended into dance. This too is part of Modern Educational Dance. It is also part of theatre and so has great importance in the dance drama lesson. The vigour that boys bring to physical education can be recaptured in dramatic movement and the skills and disciplines of physical education applied. Providing dance drama stories offer vigorous masculine qualities, boys will enjoy it as much as girls.

There are four ways of tackling dance drama, apart from the dance which comes within a story.

1 The class listens to a piece of music and creates a story to fit the music.
2 The class chooses or creates a story and then finds the music to fit the changing moods, scenes, or characters.
3 The class is given a stimulus, works out a story and then tries to fit it to the music, *eg*, A Sword, story about Revenge and a duel. Music *Zorba's Dance*.
4 A mimed activity such as washing-up is extended into drama, by allowing the movements to grow and flow into each other, accompanied by music.

Some teachers may prefer to start with mimed stories to music. *A Christmas Carol* is an example which suits the 9 to 15 age group. It would be a pity, however, not to provide some opportunity for improvisation with speech within the term's work. Improvisations around the theme of *A Christmas Carol* could form an introduction to the dance drama of the story.

LESSON PLANNING

The lessons which follow show the early planning stages in exercise form and refer to unstreamed classes. Until the class has developed a fair amount of self-control and the ability to work and discuss in harmony, with a good degree of sincerity, they appear quite satisfied to approach the story in this way. Some classes may need more lessons with the preliminary approach, while others may be able to go on and develop the story in full with individual and group casting. This is a progression which comes with the development of the group. The following examples show that the lesson scheme is always complete in itself and however short the lesson, the class should always have the satisfaction of feeling they have achieved success in what they have done. Also, that they have explored some area of human experience a little deeper and be a little wiser for it. The following lessons were used and developed with actual classes and therefore have a quality which was real for that class and the planning followed their development. These lesson plans are intended to act as a guide only.

The sample scheme that follows is divided into activities. In this way there is full class participation all the time. Each child is able to try on various roles and so is able to contribute to the final discussion from both points of view. When the story presents possibilities for movement this is allowed for, the aim being to encourage a certain quality of movement within their personal style. The rats for example, if helped to listen to the music and think of its movement qualities can contribute their own ideas, *eg* fat lazy rats with stretching movements or quick, long nosed, curious shuffling rats. The time spent in listening to the music and finding the right words is very valuable as it is a direct aid to language development, especially if it is possible to note the words the class suggest and recall them in another lesson, when having felt the sensation of 'long nosed, curious, shuffling', the written words become more meaningful and the spoken word expressive. Whenever possible the young people should be presented with or encouraged to create for themselves, situations where language is used for many different purposes, not only for playing with words and sounds, but for description, instruction, persuasion, defence, comfort, release, emotional communication and factual reporting.

When crowd scenes are possible in the story, they enable the shy child to experiment with words without embarrassment. They also encourage a sensitivity between members of the group and provide opportunities for climax of sound. Very often a crowd scene is not the uncontrolled mob it appears to be. The changing moods of the crowd within the story make each child use its own self-control to achieve group success, *eg* the angry crowd around the Mayor and his Councillors are compelled to change their mood by the entrance of the Pied Piper. This demands sincerity and concentration as well as self-control.

Sometimes the story offers the teacher a chance to plan work in pairs or small groups. These groups work simultaneously, spaced out round the hall. In this way, sincerity is encouraged and the lesson becomes an experiment rather than a show. Similarly, the story may offer a chance for the child to work as an individual but again the members of the class would participate simultaneously.

Within any carefully planned framework, there must be a chance for the child to create for himself or he will merely lean on the teacher's creativity and the work will lose its value.

The activities themselves may provide enough satisfaction for a class just beginning this work, but the possibilities for further development would be to cast and set acting areas round the hall, put the music on to tape in the right order (having now judged the right amount of music for the class absorption) and then take the story as a class play in the round.

Another approach would be to take the class as a whole from the beginning and work with them through the story, allowing casting to evolve naturally by volunteers. The quality of language and sincerity of approach comes through discussion, so that a scene is 'worked on' with the teacher as leader, maybe taking part at times. If the language does not ring true, the scene stops for more discussion and another attempt is made. The teacher does not suggest words or sentences, although within the discussion he may purposely use a phrase or word he would like them to use. The danger of using the first method is that it could be merely surface work with very little depth of thought for the child and therefore not allowing them to explore any real area of human experience.

The danger of the second is that the child never gets on with the drama and loses interest in the discussion. Once the absorption is broken some children find it difficult to return.

So much depends on the personality and quick thinking of the teacher. The drama teacher should be an opportunist and be ready to seize upon something which will extend the child's experience. He should also have an awareness which tells him immediately how far he can take the group without losing their interest. Above everything he should know what are the possible values in this work and be able to present the child with the opportunity to develop along as many lines as possible.

When the drama lesson succeeds, creative energy is generated and the teacher's own energy renewed.

SAMPLE SCHEME   *The Pied Piper of Hamelin*

Approaches

The Art Specialist may present the class with an illustration, a slide or model. The Biologist may produce a stuffed or bottled rat. The English specialist may well read some of the poem, while the Musician may play the recorder. The more personal the approach, the more attractive to the child and the imagination once caught, the lesson should proceed with the teacher a confident leader. The class feel secure when the lesson progresses at a confident pace. If certain children disturb the lesson because they find absorption difficult, it is sometimes possible to stand near them when narrating. They will need extra help and encouragement, but this should be given without disrupting the rest of the class. It is sometimes possible to control through the story, *eg*, Teacher: 'It's dangerous to climb on the roof of the Town Hall! They haven't repaired it for years!'... To the boys busily climbing the P.E. apparatus... And to the group of 'rats' huddled together giggling... 'Each rat has a morsel of food for himself and makes sure he is somewhere where no one else can reach it'. After the initial discussion the lessons might take the following pattern of activities.

1 In pairs the class are spaced out round the hall. They are two villagers discussing the rats. (If some pairs find absorption difficult, the teacher's presence on their side of the room showing

helpful interest in their contribution often helps. It might also help to let that pair show to the others. If nothing worthwhile is said, and by this I mean there is no sincerity in their work, it might mean that your preliminary work was not a sufficient stimulus to enter them into the mood or minds of the people living in the village.)

2   Pairs join up to make fours or sixes and continue the discussion relating their previous conversations to each other and making some decisions. (Each group may be asked to tell their plans to the others.)

3   In pairs again. This time they are the Mayor and the Councillor discussing the rats. (If asked to label themselves A and B, the teacher can then say 'A is the Mayor and B is the Councillor. Later we'll change over'. This saves any argument and they learn to trust your choice.)

4   Change over. Now B is the Mayor. (If there are three children in one group, C can always create a further interest.)

5   One or perhaps two passages of music are played and the class listen and suggest which one would be most suitable; the words are suggested to describe the rats' movement. Then the class experiment working on their own and not coming into contact with any other rats while they try out the actions and maybe say the chosen words with the music and their own accompanying movement. (They might enjoy taking this section on its own and expanding it for the rest of the lesson, choosing words and arranging them in 'Carl Orff'* fashion, with an accompaniment of percussion or merely the words themselves.

 eg, sudden, scuffle, shuffle…(pause)…sniffling, snuffling, curious…whiff, aroma, delicious, delectable, delightful, whiff of…snap, trap, jump, scamper, hide, curl in, long nosed snout, out…sudden, scuffle, shuffle…

and so on.

The words of the poem which describe the rats have a rhythm which encourages movement.

 Rats!
 They fought the dogs, and killed the cats,
 And bit the babies in the cradles,
 And ate the cheese out of the vats,

*FURTHER REFERENCE
Music for Children,* Carl Orff & Gunild Keetman, 33 CX 1549.

And licked the soup from the cook's own ladles,
Split open the kegs of salted sprats,
Made nests inside men's Sunday hats,
And even spoiled the women's chats,
By drowning their speaking
With shrieking and squeaking,
In fifty different sharps and flats.

Into the street the Piper stept,
Smiling first a little smile,
As if he knew what magic slept
In his quiet pipe the while;
Then, like a musical adept,
To blow the pipe his lips he wrinkled,
And green and blue his sharp eyes twinkled
Like a candle flame where salt is sprinkled;
And ere three shrill notes the pipe uttered,
You heard as if an army muttered;
And the muttering grew to a grumbling;
And out of the houses the rats came tumbling.
Great rats, small rats, lean rats, brawny rats,
Brown rats, black rats, grey rats, tawny rats,
Grave old plodders, gay young friskers,
Fathers, mothers, uncles, cousins,
Cocking tails and pricking whiskers,
Families by tens and dozens,
Brothers, sisters, husbands, wives—
Followed the Piper for their lives.

6 *(a)* Work in pairs—Piper and Mayor if desired.
(b) Individual work. Each child is the Pied Piper and makes a magical entry into the Council Chamber, accompanied either by a cymbal crash which has a long sound or the beginning of *Harry Janos: The Fairy Tale Begins*. (This is in itself a movement exercise demanding from the child balance, poise and the movement and concentration, held as long as the sound can be heard.)
7 The scene in the Council Chamber. (This might well be one which you would start with and develop if you were using the whole class method. You would need to cast the Mayor and the Pied Piper, some councillors. The rest of the class would be the complaining villagers. This scene should work naturally towards

a climax and end with the Pied Piper playing his pipe and entic-
ing away the rats, having been promised a thousand guilders
for his efforts.)

8 The Piper returns and asks for his money. (This could be done
as a class, in small groups or in twos.)

9 Children are playing in the street when they hear the piper
taking his revenge upon the villagers and they leave their games
and follow him. (A recorder or *Viennese Musical Clock* from
Harry Janos. Here there is an opportunity for movement games
to music and improvisation in small groups of pairs. There is also
opportunity to use this for putting the children's point of view
forward – 'Should they have paid the piper what they promised
him?; How does the lame boy manage when it comes to playing?; What is their attitude towards him?' Here is an area of
human experience worth doing in a little depth.)

10 The lame boy returns to tell what he has seen. (In pairs and
a chance to change over, then to relate their imagined experience
to the class. Finding words for the description of the hidden
land is practice in language. The alert teacher could note poor
structure and yet praise or note imaginative language, recall this
experience and use it in another lesson.)

11 The end of the story can be created by the class. (They may
prefer to express it in movement to music, movement to silence,
or they may prefer to do it round a conference table. The
tragedy of Aberfan is a comparative example that springs to mind
and might provide some interesting discussion for older children.)

This story, depending on the way it is presented, will appeal
to any age group in the middle years. The only reservation being
that some teachers may prefer not to act, but to imagine the rats,
when working with older children.

This lesson scheme as it stands, would cover two or three
lessons, depending on the depth of any one activity, but each
individual lesson should be rounded off with some calming down
activity, relevant to the story. Personally, I think it would be a
mistake to drag a single story over a term and try to achieve
too much in the one story, when there are so many, not only in
books but in the minds of the children. Number 7 or 8/9 and
10 could well stand on their own as lesson plans. The activity
must suit not only the environment, the teacher's personal skills

and the child's development, but their experience in other fields. Geography and the coal mining industry may well have used Aberfan for discussion and at that time, the last scene in the Pied Piper may well have been the only part relevant to do in depth. The history project may have covered the Plague of London and here the villagers' dispute with the officials would have been an interesting link with literature. If the link had been with poetry then much more of the poem would have been read so that the final result would have included a feeling for Browning's rhythms and style. When a large space is unobtainable the teacher's ingenuity must provide the appropriate part of the story to suit the environment and provide the rest by narration.

The following may be among the aims of an Educational Drama lesson:

1 To improve absorption. Unless there is absorption there cannot be sincerity.

2 To develop co-operation so they can work harmoniously together.

3 To develop self-control in movement and improve its quality.

4 To develop their ability to listen and distinguish differing volumes, pitches or qualities of sound.

5 To encourage a 'flow' of improvised speech and increase the volume to that which is natural for the situation.

6 To help them 'play' their stories, developing a sense of form and dramatic climax.

7 To give them practice in climax and de-climax, both in movement and speech.

8 To give the group an opportunity to create orally together, so that one child's imagination will stimulate the imagination of others.

9 To help them organise their ideas, select and make a group decision.

10 To provide a warm-up session, which will tune them both physically and imaginatively for the work that follows.

11 To take a short episode to improvise in depth, so that discussion and thought may produce dialogue which is meaningful and sincere.

12 To make them aware of the possibilities of the human voice

to express emotions, meaning of words and atmosphere.

13   To increase their vocabulary in the scenes they have chosen to improvise.

14   To introduce them to the scripted scene in a way which will make the words more meaningful.

15   To create a piece of 'theatre' from a script or improvisation.

16   To help them to appreciate poetry, or literature in movement and words, the final shape being an art form.

17   To enable them to explore their favourite stories.

18   To allow the class to 'play out' its latest television craze; its aggression; its home problems or its social fears.

19   To provide a stimulus for creative writing or discussion.

20   To construct a situation, where they can learn about people, leading to discussion of human behaviour and motives.

21   To provide practice for social or work situations.

22   To enable them to discover themselves and their own reactions under certain pressures.

23   To increase their awareness of the problems of the world or the society in which we live.

24   To allow them to identify with characters from the past and so come to a greater understanding of our social history.

25   To extend a project.

26   To plan a situation where language is used for a specific purpose such as factual reporting.

27   To use acting games which will help to increase the group's sensitivity towards each other.

28   To experience the joy of creation.

Beginning work in a hall or large empty classroom with 9 to 11 year olds

This lesson is for children who have not had any movement work for some time or who have had restricted drama in a classroom where a small space at the front was the only acting area. When confronted with a large area, they need a lesson which will encourage them to explore the space, to use it imaginatively, to work with other members of the class without obstructing or annoying them, to control their movement and be helped by sounds for which they have to listen carefully.

Imaginative playground games also demand a flexible use of space, and the ritual aspect of movement and speech encourages self-control. If the class work well together in a team situation, such games would make an excellent beginning. However, if the children are likely to become over excited when introduced to drama in a large space, the teacher may feel more confident beginning with the following lesson, which keeps the situation sectionally controlled while still allowing a certain amount of creative freedom. After a few lessons along these lines, dramatic playground games might be very successful as introduction material.

Ideally, but not necessarily, the space should be blacked out and illuminated with either white or coloured spots. The 'theatrical' or 'discotheque' appearance, however odd to the adult, sets a scene which suggests interesting experiment and challenge, rather than a place to fool about.

Certain rules may be agreed upon, such as correct clothing and non-slip footwear; not to use the stage or curtains until later in the term; that if a tunnel is needed, chairs should be put out especially and not to use a tunnel of stacked chairs which surround the hall; that rostra should be lifted and not dragged, and for safety's sake no one should hide under a box; that one group does not disturb or take a box belonging to another group. The teacher's signal to stop should be explained.

Simple rules will ensure that no one is hurt and that arguments and mischievous behaviour are limited.

THE PLANNING

1 Walk anywhere in the room and look at things carefully. Examine their shape as if you had seen them for the first time. Become aware of how they feel when you touch them – some things are cooler than others...some smoother...examine something which you notice is very tiny...and now a large object... continue on your own and stop when you hear this signal (drum).

2 Now find a partner and work together on this. Talk to each other about your discoveries...(signal is given)...remember to stop when you hear the signal, because it means we will go on to the next idea.

3 This time I am going to bang the drum making different rhythms. I want you and your friend to stay together and move with the same rhythm as the drum. When I give a very loud bang. I want you to change your direction, but be careful not to bump into any other couple.

...(slow walking rhythm) BANG...(skipping rhythm) BANG ...(Indian hunt rhythm) BANG...etc.

4 Now work on your own again. You need a circle of space around you. When I bang the drum I want you to make yourself as wide as you can. Now as tall as you can. Now as small. Now as long as you can. Hold it still until I bang the drum again... try again a little faster. Make yourself as wide as you can...as small as you can...as tall as you can...as long as you can...just relax.

5 This time, when I bang on the drum I want you to choose for yourself which position you'll take.

6 Now listen to the sound of the cymbal. Put up your hand when you can no longer hear it. Now choose again, but this time you go from one position to the other very slowly, using all the sound. Listen...the sound has only just finished and some of

you were already there. Try again and use all the sound. Now change to the next position...and again...and lastly...good.

7 Find your partner again. This time I am going to play some music and I want you to imagine you are playing a ball game. Just decide which one you'll choose...When the music stops I want to see if you can stop at exactly the same time...as if the camera had taken a film of you and this was the snapshot which had been developed. Stand very still so that you can hear the first notes of the music, but have a good beginning position, again as if a film had been taken.

8 This time I shall change the music occasionally and instead of being fast, it will be quite slow. Instead of a snapshot we have the film running in slow motion. Just try for a moment and move in slow motion...now try and throw a ball...control the movement all the way through the throw...good. Now try with the music. (Music alternates here, either a tape is used or a twin turntable record player or two separate record players.)

9 Now sit down and listen to this music (*Pizzicata* from *Sylvia*). What did it suggest to you? (all ideas are accepted). Choose one of these ideas and get ready to begin. Work on your own this time. Get a good beginning position and have a moment's silence before we begin....

10 (To one child in the class)...You were chasing a mouse in an attic! Am I right? I thought so. Can you describe the attic for us?...etc.

11 (As a de-climax, or calming down process, the class quietly exchange descriptions of the story they had experienced and then in some way this is linked to the next lesson.)

FURTHER REFERENCE
A Chance for Everyone John Hodson and Peter Slade, Cassell.
Exploration Drama—Carnival William Martin and Gordon Vallins, Evans.
Children's Games Street and Playground Iona and Peter Opie, Oxford University Press.
Drama in Education. Students' conclusions at the Institute of Education, University of Newcastle upon Tyne 1966-67, under the direction of Dorothy Heathcote.

Beginning work in a hall or
large empty classroom with 12 to 14 year olds

When beginning drama with this age group it is more important than ever to move from the known to the unknown, so I have suggested a variety of approaches, which should eventually lead (some classes taking longer than others), to a more creative approach to the subject. The teenager is embarrassed at getting up in a large space in front of his friends. Again, the homely psychedelic lighting can help to overcome this. Once they have established that the teacher is confident and will not laugh at or criticise their efforts, they will enter into the work with obvious enjoyment. By fourteen, some youngsters have already inter- nalised their play and no longer feel the need to act out a scene which they can visualise quite well in their imagination. This should be respected, but participation encouraged because it is a group activity. However, when any opportunity arises, those youngsters may well enjoy the projected play of sound and lighting. The creative use of the tape recorder and scripting, appeal to this age group.

MOVEMENT ACTIVITIES WITH AN ADULT SLANT

1 *Working in a supermarket*
Members of the class will have sat themselves around the edge of the room, boys separated from girls; so the activity starts with them sitting at the adding machines as the customers come past. They might need to move their chairs a little, but nothing drastic is asked at this stage. The music used could be *Cobbler's Song* from *Chu, Chin Chow* which has a 'ting' every so often, or *Steptrotters* by the Shadows. As the music continues, the teacher

as narrator, suggests that as there are no customers at the moment, the manager has asked them to go and arrange a basket of tins out on the shelves. If they have been able to get into the mood of the situation through your setting, they will now begin to get up and move about. They may need more narration from you to guide their early attempts.

> *eg* It's nearly coffee break (they automatically speed up). Oh lord, you've put them on the wrong shelf (they move to another area).
>
> It's that one over there!
>
> You hate this job (slow bored movements).
>
> You quite like this job. You like arranging things artistically (demands happy concentration).
>
> You find a tin without a label (choice of next step...).

and so on....

The activity should have an ending which will encourage them to be in the place where you will start your next idea.

> *eg* The manager has asked you to carry one of the boxes out of the store room and stack it in the centre of the store and wait. (If chairs are indicated as boxes and the music finishes just as they reach the centre, you are ready for the next step, which might be...)
>
> Move into pairs. One of you is the manager. He says that he didn't tell you to bring the box. Argue with him. Now change over....
>
> You are all the assistant again. The manager has told you to move the boxes back again or you'll get your cards.
>
> (Music is added. Choice is left for them to make their own decision. Discussion may follow on working conditions and unreasonable employers.)

2   Drugs

This might be a theme for discussion in the English lesson. Electronic music may stimulate a desire to attempt slow motion movement, as if under the influence of drugs, or in a dream. This age group can achieve great sensitivity to such music and they are capable of producing movement which reacts to sound in such a way that it becomes dance. To add a vocal effect which matches the sound and their own movement, is a challenge which they enjoy trying to meet. *Aquarius* from the musical *Hair*, can be obtained on an E.P. and adds a vocal which sets the mood. Also, from the same show is the song entitled *Walking in Space.*

3 Fights

Leading on from Section 2, or perhaps they might come beforehand, are fight sequences. Fights rehearsed in slow motion, carefully planned to numbers or drum beats, demand concentration and movement which is controlled, but masculine and dynamic.

eg In pairs – class members fight with imaginary swords (long sweeping movements) or knives (sharp, small thrusts) or heavy clubs (weighty, wheeling objects) or fists. Whatever the choice for the class, they need to practise balance and concentration.

(a) To ten drum beats, work out ten attacks and hold each one until the next sound.

(b) Now try to be more adventurous and move around the room at the same time. Be aware of levels, balance, length of weapon, weight of weapon, etc.

(c) Now count to yourselves and try it without any drum beats.

(d) One of you is wounded in the middle of the fight, but goes on and eventually is victorious. Work that out as a continuation of the first sequence.

4 Dance drama

Dance drama to music such as *Slaughter on Tenth Avenue* or *West Side Story* can grow out of such work. A good story line or a study of relationships helps these young people to express themselves in movement as well as speech.

IMPROVISATION WITH MUSIC AS MOOD BACKGROUND

1 The Market

Here is a scene familiar to practically everyone. Stalls can be set up and the members of the class buy or sell, call out their wares and people flow easily from one stall to another. Then the scene is started again, but this time perhaps a child steals an apple and a chase ensues. Here music could accompany the chase. *Trisch Trasch Polka* played at 78. The control of the situation is the music. The music stops, the class freezes. A little more

could now be added. The teacher stops the music when 'the
thief' is caught and a crowd scene follows involving the police.
The ending is left for the class to decide. The music has helped
the chase and avoided horse play in which 'the thief' could
have been hurt, but in the final repeat, when all the action has
been linked together, the class no longer needs to freeze, but
stops in a controlled manner, natural for the situation.

2 Coffee bar
A social drama situation. In the coffee bar a number of events
could take place.... Two gangs meet and maybe quarrel; a robbery might be planned; a group may decide how best to stop a
gang terrorising the area; there could be an accident outside and
they find the telephone kiosk has been wrecked; another group
might discuss how to make a success of the church jumble sale;
or it might be simply a scene where people, previously unknown
to each other come together and talk. The juke box in the background sets the authentic mood, but also highlights the effects of
silence when it is switched off.

3 Ship in a storm at sea
Sound effects such as thunder, wind or *Mars* from the *Planet
Suite,* give a very suitable background for a scene where speech
needs to be loud and prolonged to give the right effect. The
contrast when the storm is over can be obtained from Benjamin
Britten's *Sea Interludes* or just *Seagulls and Wash.*

WORKING FROM A SCRIPTED SCENE

Doctor and the Devils Dylan Thomas's film script makes ideal
study for adaptation into dialogue, with a view to adding improvisation in the crowd scenes, especially those in the market and
the public house.

Having read the dialogue they would be able to try out in
pairs scenes which the film scenario omitted and which we have
to fill in in our imaginations, *eg* the conversation between Broom
and Fallon in the Pub, before they went over to entice Jenny and
Alice and the trial scene. A chorus of voices which come to him
at the end of the play, each taunting him about the events for
which he was indirectly responsible, could be an interesting exer-

cise in creativity, which could then be taped with a musical background.

The following scenes have been adapted by Robin N. Pemberton-Billing, Director of the Octagon Theatre, Bolton.

DOCTOR AND THE DEVILS SCENE 4

A Tavern. On a bench in a corner sit two men. No one sits quite next to them though the tavern is crowded. We recognise them as the two men of the graveyard. Both are drunk, though solemnly as befits men whose business is death.
*The top-hatted man (*PRAYING HOWARD*) has an almost benevolent, almost sweet and saintly appearance, run to seed and whisky. The short man (*MOLE*) is very hairy; almost furry, like a mole. They raise their tankards to each other.*

MOLE   To the dead!

PRAYING HOWARD   To the Surgeons of our City!

They drink.
Now we see, sitting quite close to them, the two men of the Market place. They are listening hard, but cautiously, to the other three.

MOLE   It's been a good month. I'm thirsty.
PRAYING HOWARD   A blessed month.
MOLE   Subjects like penny pies. Plenty of 'em. I'm thirsty too, I've drunk three pints o' gin. And I'm goin' to drink three pints more....
PRAYING HOWARD   Careful, careful, you'll get the taste for it.

And both of them croak and laugh, without smiling, like two carrion crows.
FALLON *and* BROOM *are listening.*
The short, squat man beckons, secretly, with a stubby black finger, to an old woman, all rags and bones, standing drinking near them.

Coming closer, we hear his whisper:
FALLON   Who would they be with all that money for the drink?

The woman looks, with frightened eyes, at the croakers in the corner. Then she whispers:

WOMAN   Praying Howard, and *(her voice goes softer)*...the Mole.

And the squat man questions her again, in a rough, Irish whisper:

FALLON   And what do they do for a living, my lovely?

She answers, in a sharp whisper full of fear:
WOMAN   Body-snatchers.

He makes a movement as though to cross himself, then lets his hand fall, and looks at his companion.
We see the thin side-twisted lips of his companion frame the syllables:

BROOM   Body-snatchers.

They look at each other.
The attention of audience is drawn to MURRAY *and* BROWN
(a young student doctor) they are both a little drunk.

BROWN   Refined gathering tonight.
MURRAY   Thomas was on top of the world.
BROWN   Gracious, loquacious, insulting, exulting...avuncular, carbuncular.
What did he talk about at dinner, apart from sex and religion and politics?
MURRAY   Body-snatchers.

BROWN, *with a 'Sh!' of warning, gives* MURRAY *a dig with his elbow, and nods up the room to where the* MOLE *now solemnly pouring whisky down* PRAYING HOWARD.
As MURRAY *looks in their direction, so he sees the beautiful girl and beckons her over to him.*
Beautifully unsteady, she approaches. BROWN *and* HARDING
squeeze up to make room for her beside MURRAY.

MURRAY   Sit down and drink with us, sweet Jenny Bailey, my lovely charmer.

NELLY   Look at Jenny Bailey, the lady. Drinking with the doctor. Look at her Kate.

KATE   I'd like to be putting my nails in her eyes...I saw that Bob Fallon looking at her yesterday. Mind your step, Nelly.

NELLY   She won't be young for long. Another year and the men won't look at her. She's the sort that grows old in a night.

I seen your Mr Broom looking at her, too. Showing all his teeth.

KATE   She wouldn't go with Fallon or Broom, not she. Look at her. Not when there's money.

MURRAY   Why can't we meet in another place, sometimes, Jennie? Anywhere else, not always in this damned tavern, with all the sluts and drunks staring at us.

JENNIE   Where else could you take me, sweetheart, except for a walk in the fields—and in winter too! Kissing in a hedge in the snow like two robins.

MURRAY   We could find somewhere to be together.

JENNIE   Loving in the lanes, with all the trees dripping down your back and the thorns tearing your petticoats, and little insects wriggling, all over you—oh no! Or sitting holding hands in your lodgings all the evening, and your brother studying books in the corner! *(Softly)* You know you could come home with me.

MURRAY   And you know that I won't. I can't. Don't you understand that I couldn't go back with you there. Not there, in that house. I don't want to think of you in that house, ever. I don't want to think of the others, and your smiling at them and letting them....

JENNIE   Oh, the 'others' don't mean a thing in the wide world. They're different. I'm for you. Come back; now. I'll tell Rosie you're staying and....

MURRAY   No. No, Jennie. Please. You're beautiful. Come away. Come away from everything here. Are you never going to say 'Yes' to me, even if I ask you a thousand thousand times! I'm asking you again, Jennie.

JENNIE   *(Gaily)* Oh a fine young doctor's wife I'd make. Wouldn't the ladies love me? 'And from what part do you come, Mrs Murray?' 'Number 23, Pigs' Yard. Your husband used to call on Wednesdays'....

Cut to the door of the tavern, where the two men of the

Grass-market, the tall, thin, always half-dancing one, and the
square one, enter. They look round the room.
They see KATE *and* NELLY, *and make their way across the*
crowded swirling bar towards them.
The tall one crackles his way through the crowd, jumping
and finger-snapping, a long damp leer stuck on the side of his
face. The squat one elbows his way through, now sullenly
truculent, now oily and almost bowing.
They stand over their women.
And the squat man says, ingratiatingly and yet with an under-
menace:

BROOM   Can you buy a little drink for us, Nelly darling? We're
thirsty, love.

And the thin mans says, in his high, mad voice:

FALLON   Can you buy a little drink for Fallon and Broom,
Fallon and Broom....

He makes the grotesque movements of drinking, still finger-
snapping, one shoulder higher than the other.

NELLY   There's money for two and that's all. Here, buy 'em
yourself, Bob Fallon.

She tosses FALLON *a coin. And as he catches the coin and*
shoulders the few steps to the bar, BROOM *reaches for* NELLY'S
drink. NELLY *makes as if to snatch the tankard back, but*
BROOM *suddenly shows his teeth and pretends to snap at her.*

KATE   Ach, leave him be. Broom's got the devil in him tonight.
He'd bite your hand through. I know him.

By this time FALLON *has returned with two drinks, and hands*
one to BROOM, *who attacks it hungrily again.*

FALLON, *from under his heavy, hanging eyebrows, stares around*
the bar. Suddenly he sees MERRY-LEES *and the two others.*

FALLON   *(To the women)* There's the three... *(His voice*
lowers)   snatchers we see in the 'Old Bull'. They're swillin'
the drink again. Must've digged up another tonight.

He turns to look at Broom, who is staring at the three
Resurrectionists with glinting, unseeing eyes.

FALLON   Fourteen pounds for a corpse they get when it's digged up new.... Fourteen pounds!...

BROOM   (*In his high, loud voice*) Fourteen pounds for gin and pies....

KATE   Hush! you mad dog....

NELLY   There's no more left.

She gets up and goes towards the door. FALLON *follows her,* BROOM *and* KATE *behind him. As they move through the bar to the door, we hear* FALLON *whine:*

FALLON   Come on, Nelly darlin', scrape up a penny or two for drop for us.... There's plenty of ways, lovely....

All four exit from the tavern.
NELLY *walks to a barrow just outside the pub and takes the handles.*
The barrow is heaped with rags.
FALLON, BROOM *and* KATE *follow her as she begins to push the wheel-barrow through the moonlit Market.*
Suddenly, with a yelp, BROOM *leaps on to the barrow, sitting bolt upright among the rags.*

BROOM   (*In a high, gay snarl*) Broom
In his carriage and pair....

Nelly takes no notice but doggedly pushes the barrow on. And sullenly FALLON *walks at the side,* KATE *trailing after him.*

FALLON   Fourteen pounds for a corpse!....

They move out of the Market, through the alleyways.

NELLY   (*In a harsh grumble as she trundles the barrow on with its load of rags and one cackling man*) Why don't you dig one up yourself? You're frightened of the dark....

Over the cobbles of lonely alleys the barrow rattles, and the finger-snapping, dog-haired man squatting on the rags points his finger at one dark doorway, then at another.

BROOM   They're dead in there.... Dig 'em up, Fallon.... In there.... In there.

Round a corner they come into Rag-and-Bone Alley.

SCENE 8

Market Place *A lively market scene.* FALLON, BROOM, KATE *and*
NELLY *enter.* FALLON *hands* NELLY *and* KATE *some money.*

FALLON'S VOICE   For you, Nelly love. All for yourself. For you,
Kate.
Now, still closely, we see the four at the table.
FALLON   Broom and I share the rest.

And FALLON *divides, in one movement of his broad fingers like
big toes, the remaining coins.*
BROOM *snatches his coins up.*

NELLY   (*Softly, in a kind of drunken, lumpish amazement*)
Seven pounds ten for an old man....
FALLON   Oh, the shame that he wasn't a young man....

*And, with their own kinds of laughter, they walk round the
market.* FALLON *and* BROOM *are looking at the wares on a
clothes-stall. They plough and scatter through the clothes,
while the stall-keeper, a fat woman smoking a pipe, looks on
expressionlessly.* FALLON *pulls out a shawl from a heap of
oddments and tosses a coin to the woman who, still
expressionlessly but with the deftness of a trained seal,
catches it.*

FALLON   I'll have this....

He pulls out another shawl, and a skirt, and a petticoat.
FALLON   and...this...and this...and this...

And BROOM *has decked himself with lace from the stall and
is mincing around in the parody of a drunken woman.*
FALLON, *with a wide, extravagant gesture, piles all his
presents under his arm, and tosses the woman another coin.
She catches it. And* BROOM *still prances, now with a bonnet
on his head.*

BROOM   Look at me...look at me. My mother wouldn't know me.

And FALLON *and* BROOM *link arms and move away through the
Market,* BROOM *in his fineries,* FALLON *trailing a shawl behind*

him in the mud of the cobbles.
Arm in arm they move on through the Market, to the distant
playing of a fiddle.

SCENE 11

Tavern. *Many of the faces are familiar to us now. That old bag*
of female bones over there, she was the one who described to
FALLON *and* BROOM *the profession of* MOLE, *that fat woman*
with a pipe there, who tosses down her drink as a tamed
seal swallows a fish, she was the one who kept the stall
where FALLON *and* BROOM *bought clothes for their women;*
that humpback there, looking at everything with an idiot
smile, he is the one called BILLY BEDLAM; *one of those two*
very young men over there, being wise and waggish to a pretty
girl of sixteen, is the student BROWN; *that tall man in a*
scarecrow's top-hot, hiccuping solemnly, he is the one called
ANDREW MERRY-LEES; *and there are others we have seen before;*
in the tavern, in the street, in the Market, all of them,
in their way, vice-residents of the tavern; and among them a
few honest, very poor people.
A dark, pretty young woman with a sulky expression, seated
at the far end of the room, waves her hand.
And we see JENNIE BAILEY, *in her gay shawl, charming her way*
down the room, being familiar with everyone (including
BILLY BEDLAM) *and over-familiar with some.*
Now we see that JENNIE BAILEY *is sitting next to the dark young*
woman.
JENNIE *drinks from the dark girl's drink.*

JENNIE   I been to see the play in the theatre, Alice.
ALICE   You didn't see no play, dear. You been up High Street.
JENNIE   I did. From the outside. Who shall we get to buy us a drink?

She roves her eye round the pub. She nods towards BILLY
BEDLAM.

JENNIE   Him?

She nods towards BROWN. *He catches her glance, is about
to blush, then, remembering his age, winks back.*

JENNIE   Him!
She smiles at BROWN, *beckons him over. He comes over.*

JENNIE   Going to buy us some medicine, Doctor?
BROWN   Oh, of course I am, Jennie....
JENNIE   Some for Alice and some for me? It's a cold night for
poor working girls like us....

BROWN *goes off.*

JENNIE   I saw my Doctor at the theatre. In my box.
ALICE   John Murray?

JENNIE *nods.*

ALICE   Why d'you treat the poor creature so badly, Jennie?
JENNIE   Oh, but Alice darling, I'm so very fond of him. I like
him better than any man in the whole world....
ALICE   Then why d'you carry on in front of his eyes and....
JENNIE   Oh, but I don't, I don't....
ALICE   ...and teasing him that he's a parson's son, and letting
him see you walk out with any Tom, Dick, and Harry....
JENNIE   ...I don't know any Harry....
ALICE   ...No one could know you loved him, you're so brazen,
dear....
JENNIE   Oh, I want some fun before I die.... You're a parson's
daughter yourself.... He must love me for what I am, that's all
there is....

BROWN *comes back with two mugs.*

JENNIE   There, you can always tell, he's got a sweet face.... I
do like students and doctors and....
ALICE   ...butchers and bakers and candlestick-makers....

We hear a high yelping laugh, and then FALLON'S *voice.*

FALLON'S VOICE   And there's my darling Jennie....
BROOM'S VOICE   And mine, and mine!

And FALLON *and* BROOM *stagger to the table, pushing* BROWN
aside. FALLON *pulls a bottle out of his pocket.*

FALLON   Who's going to share a bottle with two county gentle-
men?
FALLON *and* BROOM *sit themselves next to* ALICE *and* JENNIE,
FALLON *next to* JENNIE, BROOM *to* ALICE. FALLON *pulls two
mugs across the table, and fills them.*

JENNIE   I never drink with strangers except on Mondays....
FALLON   And it's Monday tonight.
O the stars are shining, the bells are chiming, we'll drink to
Monday and Tuesday and....

FALLON *pours out another drink.*

JENNIE   And I never drink twice with strangers before twelve
o'clock.
FALLON   And Lord, it's after twelve.
O the moon is singing, the grass is growing. We'll drink to twelve
o'clock...and one o'clock...and two o'clock....

FALLON *and* JENNIE *are now very tipsy.*
BROOM *is smiling, leering, giggling, and clowning to* JENNIE.
ALICE *still remains comparatively sober, and still sulky.*

FALLON   (*Wheedling*) I got two more bottles in my little room,
Miss Pretty Bailey. Two great bottles of dancin' dew that'll make
you think the sun's shining in the middle of the night...and
satiny shining couches for all the kings and queens to be lying
on.... And....
ALICE   We're not going.
JENNIE   Will you give me a diamond ring and a golden bracelet
and...
FALLON   I'll give you a bucketful of pearls. We'll sing and dance.
We'll be merry as crickets in Rag-and-Bone Alley....
JENNIE   (*Half-laughing, half-singing*) We'll be merry as crickets
in Rag-and-Bone Alley....
ALICE   (*In an angry whisper to* JENNIE) You're not going with
these two creatures.... You must wait for John·Murray.... Don't
drink any more with that Bob Fallon....
BROOM   I'll cook you liver and lights....
JENNIE   Will you cook a partridge for me?....
FALLON   And I'll put a peacock's feathers in your hair....
JENNIE   Oh, listen to them both.... You'd think they were great

rich men with crowns and palaces, not a couple of naughty tinkers....

ALICE   We're not going....

Street. *Four figures move through the Market:* FALLON, JENNIE, BROOM, ALICE. FALLON *and* JENNIE *are singing.*

FALLON AND JENNIE   We'll be merry as crickets in....

SCENE 24

Newspaper office. *Crowd noise from outside.*
The FIRST REPORTER *is writing at a table.*
The SECOND REPORTER *is walking up and down the room and glancing, every few minutes, out of the window.*

SECOND REPORTER   Was Rod smiling when he said that?
FIRST REPORTER   *(Without looking up)* If you call it smiling.
SECOND REPORTER   What did he look like?
FIRST REPORTER   *(Briefly, as he writes)* The Devil himself.
SECOND REPORTER   And Fallon?
FIRST REPORTER   Quite quiet. Vurry polite.
SECOND REPORTER   And the woman?
FIRST REPORTER   Sober.

The crowd noise rises.

SECOND REPORTER   What are you calling the article?
FIRST REPORTER   Justice.
SECOND REPORTER   *(At the window)* They're running down the street now.... Thousands of them....
Broom! Broom! Broom.... d'you hear them?
FIRST REPORTER   Broom'll go free.
SECOND REPORTER   *(Still looking out of the window)* There's another fire over Newington way...somewhere near Rock's place.... D'you hear them?
FIRST REPORTER   *(Writing, not looking up)* They won't call Rock as a witness. That'll be taken care of....

A great cry from the crowd outside....

SECOND REPORTER   D'you hear that?
FIRST REPORTER   I'm not deaf. They're nearing the end now....

DISCUSSION OF FILMS OR TELEVISION SERIALS

For those adolescents who find the written word a bore and television 'a god', a discussion of a film can often stimulate dramatic activity. If the class have been asked to watch it the previous night, there will be a good chance that everyone will at least have heard about it, if they have not actually watched it. Discussion might include the social aspects, the characters, the mood, the tension, the dramatic effects possible on film, the value of close-up etc. One could then discuss the difficulties of the stage director in the live theatre. Part of the scene could then be tried by the class. Then the language and characters discussed and perhaps re-tried. This puts the emphasis on theatre and popular entertainment. However, another time one could take the social aspect alone and extend the scene, thus concentrating on personal development.

ACTING GAMES

Instead of merely verbalising a structured situation, some young people in this age range may prefer to start with acting games. Here two or three perform in front of the class, but the situation is 'open ended'. The idea is not to see who can be the most original, but to respond immediately to a stimulus.

eg There are two chairs. One person sits on one of the chairs. Without discussion or previous planning, the second person enters and starts a scene. In doing this he implies, though perhaps not at once, the place of the scene, the character of the other person and the mood. The other person behaves and replies appropriately and the scene continues. Later a third person may come in and change the situation and characterisations already established, by creating a fresh stimulus or remark. Thus a completely new scene is begun.

Another example is the game of 'Blocking'. So often in real life a conversation or relationship is blocked from time to time by either party. An awareness of this allows a fascinating study of real life.

eg A boy tries to date a girl for a visit to the cinema. The girl continually blocks his attempts in her own personal way.

Alternatively, she responds favourably to all his remarks and the date is arranged.

Status in everyday life is also a fascinating topic for discussion and there are many games and clowning activities to illustrate this.

eg Two young people. One boosts his own status by criticising the other, who accepts the criticisms meekly. Through a case of mistaken identity, the status of a man in a position of great importance is placed upon an unsuspecting person.

Many similar games can be found in an American book entitled *Improvisation for the Theater* by Viola Spolin, published by North Western University Press.

FURTHER REFERENCE
Teaching Drama by R. N. Pemberton-Billing and J. D. Clegg, University of London Press.
Improvisation by John Hodgson and Ernest Richards, Methuen.
Exploration Drama – Routes and Horizons by William Martin and Gordon Vallins, Evans.
Theatre-Go-Round, Keith Johnstone, Royal Shakespeare Company.

Beginning in the classroom

When space is limited and concentration does not come easily to the class, ten minute sessions are preferable to a long period of drama. Any lesson may provide the stimulus or present the opportunity for activities which will develop the following.
Observation of detail.
Observation of behaviour.
Concentration.
Co-operation.
Organisation of ideas and decision making.
Stimulation of the imagination.
Training in social behaviour.
An awareness of the senses.

If the activities are related to the lesson, they will have more impact than if they are isolated suggestions from the teacher. The following are examples of short sessions taken from actual lessons.

1 Observation of detail
Lesson—English—11 year olds The class discussed the newspaper report in the local paper, of a witness who claimed that she had seen a man walking down the road in a suspicious manner and was able to recall every move he had made. The class was then asked to try to remember what the teacher did when he first entered the room to take the lesson. Each child then tried to recall, to the person sitting next to them, exactly what each had done when they got up that morning. One child went to the door and entered, making a series of definite movements on his journey to the front. The class was then asked to list in detail everything he had done.

2   *Observation of behaviour*
Lesson—English—13 year olds They had been collecting photographs or paintings of faces out of magazines. Their project was 'People'. They examined in detail the lines on the faces, the style of hair and clothes. They assessed the amount of personal care taken, habits and possible environment. The children having studied one picture in detail attempted to become that person for a few moments and then asked each other questions and attempted to answer in character.

3   *Concentration*
Lesson—Literature—9 year olds Story: *The Wonderful Adventures of Nils* by Selma Lagerlöf (translation published by J. M. Dent and Sons Limited). The class members acted to the words of the following passages while seated at their desks.

20 March...Nils is alone. Suddenly he hears a slight noise, he listens, then sees in the mirror his grandmother's handsome old chest and astride the edge an elf looking down at the finery. The boy was not scared—not of one so small. But it might be fun to play a trick on the elf. The boy snatched up the butterfly net and caught him in one sweep.
21-27 March...The night became dismal and cold. Nils didn't dare sleep because then he might fall.
9-15 April...Nils is tempted to buy the magnificent goods spread out in front of him.
5-6 May...Nils is caught at the bottom of the fisherman's basket and struggles to get out, eventually doing so.
October...Nils sets off to find something to eat. He discovers a currant bush and a fine red apple which he cuts into small pieces.
...Nils helps the new horse to get a knife out of his hoof. He cannot do it himself so carves on the hoof 'Take the iron out of the foot'.
...Nils now big fondles the wild geese and then watches them as they fly up into the sky.

4   *Co-operation*
Lesson—Poetry—15 year olds   The project has been War Poetry. The discussion had approached the subject of the traumatic conditions which stimulated the poets to write. The Desert

was chosen as an area of experience recently publicised with the Arab/Israeli war. The record *The Painted Desert* by Grofé was played to the class and in groups they were asked to write down words which sprung to mind.

eg water; heat; sand and sun.
Then their emotions or personal thoughts,
eg, can't go on; they're just behind us; it's no use; the sand's so hot; Mary; Jim; can't see; vultures waiting, waiting, waiting.

These groups then organised the words in any way they chose, sometimes repeating a word. They discussed which sounds presented the best image and so were selective. The finished product read by one of each group was individual, sincere and at times quite moving.

5 *Organisation of ideas and decision making*

Lesson—10 year olds The last fifteen minutes of a lesson taken for another teacher where work was set and which the class had finished early. Story making: Members of the class jotted down on a piece of paper something they would like to include in a story. The papers were folded and placed in a tin. Then five were taken out and read as follows:

spies
submarine
some children
ghosts
a wedding

The task now was to create a story with the class from this rather difficult selection. If it had been suggested orally it might have read...spies; submarine; island; treasure and sword, the boys winning the day and much less of a challenge than the original one.

The class sat informally for this, as near the teacher as possible, so that now the suggestions could come easily without a mad flurry of hands or shouting, which would make a call to order necessary. Decisions were made and agreed upon.

eg the reality of the ghosts and authenticity of the wedding.

6 *Stimulation of the imagination*

Lesson—Drama—10 year olds Visual and aural stimuli: the

class was shown a photograph of an old lady in a small sweet kiosk. Then they listened to the *Harry Lime Theme* played at slow speed. Then in pairs, standing by their desks, they created the characters of the old woman and a customer, miming to the music. Their first attempt being quite controlled, they then attempted it with speech; the music playing softly as a background. They were very excited and changed over to allow the other partner to play the old woman or as the boys saw her...an old man. The initial control of the music controlled the quality of the improvisation and allowed them to keep the character with some degree of sincerity.

Lesson—Drama—11 year olds The teacher had a bag full of objects, small pieces of costume and a mirror. As a crown was placed upon a head, the child looked in the mirror. Questions were asked such as 'Who are you? Where have you come from? Why are you here?' Then the children wrote what they thought, but at their own level of ability. Some wrote long sentences, while others only a word. In this lesson it was the ideas which mattered.

7 *Training in social behaviour*

Lesson—English—15 year olds Written work had involved finding press cuttings of jobs advertised and then applying for them. This lesson tackled how to behave at an interview. Discussion opened this section of the lesson and then two volunteers came to the front of the class and showed what they thought an interview would be like for the job they had written about. Again discussion followed and then in pairs sitting at their desks they all tried simultaneously. With this particular class there was some fooling about, so the teacher asked the boy concerned about his particular interests and the job for which he might be applying in the next few months. The class then tried his interview which was for an apprentice plumber. The boy then listened with the teacher and led the discussion which ended the lesson.

8 *An awareness of the senses*

Lesson—English—12 year olds Sight and Sound Poetry: the first verse of the *Blind Boy* by Colley Cibber was read to the class. An example of verse in the year 1700.

O say what is that thing called light,
Which I must ne'er enjoy;
What are the blessings of the sight;
O tell a poor blind boy!

Then they closed their eyes and tried to appreciate the texture of surfaces; discover objects near to them; walk a short distance with their eyes still closed and distinguish common sounds. Discussion then followed. Then they experimented with sight and discovered that they could look at objects in the far, near or middle distance, that sight gave them more information than mere touch, but that the two together was the best combination. They then wrote a verse replying to the boy, in similar style or one which was personal to themselves. They then considered sounds and again experimented, trying to distinguish between those sounds personal to themselves, those within the room and those outside.

The poem *Night-Piece, to Arthur Geddes,* by Edward Shanks (*Queen of China,* Martin, Secker and Warburg Ltd) was taken in the second part of the lesson.

Come out and walk. The last few drops of light
Drain silently out of the cloudy blue;
The trees are full of the dark-stooping night,
The fields are wet with dew.

All's quiet in the wood, but, far away—
Look down the hillside and across the plain—
Moves, with long trail of white that marks its way.
The softly panting train.
Come through the clearing. Hardly now we see
The flowers save dark or light against the grass,
Or glimmering silver on a scented tree
That tremble as we pass.

Hark now! So far, so far...that distant song....
Move not the rustling grasses with your feet.
The dusk is full of sounds, that all along
The muttering boughs repeat.

So far, so faint, we lift our heads in doubt.
Wind, or the blood that beats within our ears,
Has feigned a dubious or delusive note,
Such as a dreamer hears.

Again, again! The faint sounds rise and fall.
So far the enchanted tree, the song so low....
A drowsy thrush, a waking nightingale?
Silence. We do not know.

The same theme was again discussed during their literature lesson on *The Story of my Life* by Helen Keller.

FURTHER REFERENCE
Development through Drama by Brian Way, Education Today Series, Longmans.

Progression of the drama lesson
in the hall

After the initial lessons for self-control, co-operation and discovery of space, the lessons can follow a definite progression
which help the development of creativity, language and personality, especially if the teacher concerned is aware of the development in other aspects of their written and spoken English.

The length of each stage will depend upon the class concerned
and the aims the teacher has in mind. At the end of this section
is a theme for a term with older children, providing opportunities for varied dramatic or movement activities. In this way, the
teacher is still working with a sense of progression for those who
have had little drama in the primary or first year secondary, yet at
the same time the work involves activities which appeal to those
who have already progressed beyond this point and can easily
tackle the small group work with control, co-operation and
imaginative planning.

STORY INTERPRETED TO TEACHER'S NARRATION

The aims of the lesson are:

1 to practise the control signal.
2 to develop a response to climax of sound.
3 to control their movement in their own time.
4 to plan an imaginary fight in detail, developing absorption
and preventing accident or playground brawl.
5 for the class to respond individually to an imaginative stimulus, encouraging absorption.
6 to lead them into a variety of body movement, and an
imaginative use of space and level.
7 introduction to improvisation with a partner for oral descrip-

tion so that they can relate their experience to the whole class with confidence.

8 to link in theme with some other area of work already in progress.

Rostra are placed as obstacles. Chairs or P.E. equipment serve just as well. Children are asked to stand near them.

1 You are going to need a secret place, so make sure that you are on your own...you are hiding behind a wall, waiting for your gang to come past. Every now and then you peep over the top to see them. When you hear the drum beat, bob down fast and stay very still...(after one or two tries)....

2 This time we'll do the same again, but you are going to run from one hiding place to the next. Be cautious and only run when it is safe to do so. Stop very still and flatten yourself against a wall if you hear the drum beat. If you meet another person running, help them, you are their friend.

3 If you haven't already met a friend, join with one now, or a three.... This time you are hunting instead of being hunted. You are both hunting the one member of the gang who is left playing the game. Just listen to the drum (build up a climax of sound). That is when you have caught him. Imagine him this time. We'll split up later (this is repeated for quality).

4 Pick up (an imaginary) stick. When you do catch him, you pretend to be pirates with swords and have a fight. To make this look really good, it needs to be worked out in great detail. Television fights are worked out in great detail. Face your partner and I will give five beats on the drum. I want you to fight with five strokes of the sword, holding each stroke still for a moment. Think of the weight and length of the sword. Now try ten strokes. Be more adventurous. One try to escape, or maybe one of you is wounded and falls for a moment.... Now try it in your own time, count to yourselves and plan a good ending and hold it for a moment.... Now discuss what was good and try again. Label yourselves A and B.

5 Now separate so that you are quite a way apart. A is walking down a country road on his way to the gang's den; B, unknown to A, is pursuing him. He eventually catches him and they start to fight as if they were pirates with swords. Make sure you have a good ending. (Drum beat is used for stalking, climax for

attack and the ten fast beats for the fight. They may like to repeat the exercise without any sound. Speech should be encouraged on or after the attack.)

6 Now work on your own again. Find somewhere to sit which could be your room.... Your gang have played a trick on you and you are shut in this dark room. You're not afraid of the dark, but you are sure that one of your pals is hiding with you. It's a very small room, but every time you think you can see him and you pounce there's no one there.... You never catch him.... In your own time begin.... (Narration may be necessary such as) It's very dark, you think he's behind you, maybe in front, etc....

7 Now they've let you out into the bright sunshine. It's so hot and sunny that you are thinking of the holiday you had and you spread out just where you are and imagine you're in a very hot country, just sunbathing. (Sound grows in volume *Little Princess* Shadows.)

The Story

As you are lying there you see a large beach ball floating in the air like a balloon and after a time you decide you'll try to catch it. (As *Little Princess* fades *Cuckoo* grows in volume.) You can't catch it, so lie on the sand and draw with your toes. Now your finger. Now write in big letters all over the shore, on the walls of rocks or in the air...etc (sound starts to fade).

Now you are tired and decide to explore the rock pools (*Cuckoo* now fades completely and is replaced with *Les Anes*. More narration if required).

Now you see the entrance to a large cave and you explore it. (*Les Anes* now cross fades with *The Sorcerer's Apprentice*.) Suddenly you see an old chest and you manage to open it. In it are jewels and a beautiful sword. Just as you wave it in the air you are confronted by two pirates (imaginary), who demand that you fight for possession of the sword. Feeling very brave you take on two at once... (*The Sorcerer's Apprentice* cross fades with *Night on a Bare Mountain*. Eventually all music fades). Suddenly they disappear, but you still have the sword. Take it and hide it somewhere on the shore....

Now you relax on the hot sand again and dream of your adventures. You watch the red balloon floating above you until you finally close your eyes and fall asleep. (Sound of *Little Princess*

grows in volume and eventually fades.)
A slight pause....
8 (Spoken quietly) Now sit up. Find your friend again and tell them, not show them, where you hid the sword. Describe your swords to each other. Then describe the pirates.
9 Come and sit round me. What was your sword like? Tell us about your pirates, etc.
10 Next week shall we make up a story about the sword?

Further lessons following this pattern would aim to develop their sense of climax in movement and emotion, as well as sound.
 eg 1 Groups creeping out from various places and surprising another group or person with shouts of glee.
 2 Natives creating a dance to summon rain, bringing both dance and accompanying sounds to a climax.
 3 The bringing of gifts to some deity, working with the climax of music *(Mother Goose Suite, The Fairy Garden,* Ravel.)
 4 The hunter stalking his prey and eventually killing it.
Work on de-climax is equally important.
 eg 1 Having pounced on the group or person, they then joke awhile, gradually they disperse back to their original starting places.
 2 Having reached the climax of the dance, there is perhaps a moment of silence. Then the dance and sound begin again at their peak, slowly reversing the procedure until the last sound has died away.
 3 The gifts having been given, the crowd disperses.
 4 After the killing, the animal is prepared for travel, with energy almost equal to that of the attack, then in triumph it is lifted and carried home. The journey becomes slower as the burden appears heavier.

STORY CREATED BY THE CLASS AND PLANNED BY THE TEACHER (9 to 11 years)

Aims
1 to help the class organise its ideas.
2 to plan their ideas in such a way that they try out all the roles in a variety of situations.

3 to encourage greater understanding of the situation through discussion.

4 to progress from this stage to developing it as a class play with some individual casting, but mostly group casting.

Ideas
Suggested by different classes of eleven year old boys and girls.
1 *Gypsies   Boys   Stolen watch   Haunted House   Fair*
2 *Robbers   Shipwreck   Island   Treasure   Natives   Fight*
Jungle
3 *Robbers   Escape from jail   Lost in a forest   Exploring*
Caves   Guns
4 *Bonfire   night   War   Dreams   Monsters   under   the   Sea*
Trap door
5 *Frogmen   Under the Sea   Wreck   Spies   Treasure*
6 *Witches Den   Lost children*
7 *Shanty town   Spies   Empty house   Tunnel   Smuggling*
guns to Indians   Tarantula spider

As you will see, some ideas sparked off similar ones, but not always. It is often quite difficult to include all the ideas. For example the last proved quite difficult. I have chosen to give sample lessons of the first two examples.

The Story (Accidental stimulus…. Fair in town and newspaper article about a similar robbery.)
A fair was in progress in the town. Some gypsies were camped near-by. A group of children visited the fair and one of the boys discovered that his watch had disappeared. They recalled that a gypsy had bumped into them and decided that he could have stolen it. They searched the fair looking for the gypsy boy. They eventually saw him and followed him to an empty house near-by. They had heard that this house was reputed to be haunted and so entered with trepidation. They heard voices and discovered a group of gypsies playing cards and discussing what they would do with their latest load of junk. The children presumed they were speaking about stolen goods, including the watch. They were heard and a struggle ensued. They had to explain why they were there. One child escaped and went to fetch a policeman. The gypsies, indignant at being accused, frightened the children by locking them up. The policeman arrived to confront the gypsies and free the children. Each side stated their case. The

policeman asked for a description of the watch and told them it had been found on the fair ground an hour before. The gypsies were warned to keep away from the house which was private property and the children were escorted back to the road.

The Planning

1   Rostra are set up as stalls, etc. Class members become either stallholders or children at the fair. (Gay music to accompany this but speech is an essential part of the exercise.)

2   They set up a gypsy encampment and set about their normal tea-time tasks (discussion in depth is needed before this exercise so that they are really involved in the hardships and prejudice which surrounds the gypsy. Also to be discussed are the relationships of the people within the group, their attitudes to each other and to the outside world).

3   In groups of friends (ideally five or six). One is the gypsy boy. They try the scene where the boy is supposed to have stolen the watch. This is immediately followed up by the discovery and the chase.

4   Members of the class are now the children entering the supposedly haunted house. (Music...Bartok, or similar.)

5   In small groups again. The gypsies, sitting round an upturned box, discussing their latest collection of odds and ends.

6   Groups join up to form small groups of children and gypsies. The children are heard, captured and accused. They are left locked up. One escapes beforehand.

7   In small groups. 'Children' are left quite a time alone in the locked room.

8   In twos. The child has to convince the policeman that he is telling the truth.

9   (Fair music, gently fading as the scene comes to a close.) The members of the class are all workers at the fair and in their own time dismantle their equipment for the night.

Our Play (another lesson to develop these activities into a class play)

The space is arranged to provide for the fair and the house. The children are cast into groups of fair people, children and gypsies. The boy who loses his watch, the gypsy boy and the policeman are individually cast.

   The gypsies are also at the fair to begin with, only during the jostling incident do they decide to go to the house for a game of cards and a drink. During the house incident, the fair people begin to dismantle their stalls, etc. Music is used for the fair and just fades slightly during the house scene, only fading completely when the boy escapes to fetch a policeman.

The structured lesson by the teacher is but a beginning; but a beginning that can sometimes take many terms. There must be lessons where the class not only creates the story, but is able to go straight into the casting situation. They should eventually be able to set out their space, structure the story and ask for suitable music to set the mood or accompany some special movement. They may take it in sections and pause for discussion and advice. They may want to repeat for quality, but not every class can work like this immediately. Sometimes it is possible for the teacher to get inside the action at a certain point, perhaps the policeman in the example, or the leader of the gypsy encampment. Here the teacher is part of their play to act as a leader of their crowd scene, and not an actor to show them what to do or how to say something.

The Story from example No. 2

A group of men robbed a bank and managed to stow away on a ship. The ship was wrecked in a storm near an island. The stowaways managed to escape and found that they had been washed up on the sunny shore of a tropical island. In search of food, they explored the jungle and discovered natives and a golden temple. Having lost the bank money in the wreck, they decided to rob once more and that night forced their way past the guard, into the temple. However, they were caught and were about to be sacrificed to the gods, when there was a flash of lightning, followed by thunder. This was an omen to the natives who allowed the men to go. However they lost their way in the jungle and eventually collapsed, exhausted.

The Planning

1 The bank robbery. Class divides into groups of six or seven and in their own area of the hall, arrange their chairs or tables to indicate the bank, cast their robbers and plan the scene. (Each group should know how its scene will end.)
2 Still in the same group, they arrange a ship area. (Speech is

used over the effects of storm and the scene ends with them lying relaxed on the island's shore. Suitable music is *Mars* from the *Planet Suite* or *Fantasy after Dante*, followed by *Little Princess* by the Shadows. The music should cross fade. To discourage frantic swimming on the hall floor and insincere behaviour, the class members should be asked to try and show how they would be buffeted by the waves, backwards and forwards, sometimes rising, sometimes sinking and eventually coming to rest and stillness. They might practise this as an exercise on its own).

3   The journey through the jungle in pairs. (Sound effects record, *Jungle Noises* followed by drums.) Discussion of the difficulties they would encounter should precede this activity.

4   The native village. A whole class activity. (Here is a chance for the children to create within your framework. They might provide a chant, a dance or temple rites.)

5   In pairs—the two men see the Temple and decide on a plan to raid it.

6   In pairs—having escaped, they are lost in the jungle and eventually collapse (music to help extend their absorption is *Painted Desert* by Grofé or Tom Disseveldt's *Electronic Movements...Drifting*).

Our Play (another lesson, development into a class play)
Rostra are arranged to indicate the bank, the ship and the temple. The floor area is the road, sea and jungle.

    The children are divided into a large group of natives with a leader, a smaller group of sailors, a small group of bank men and customers and the two bank robbers.

    The action flows from one area to the other, the people coming to life when the appropriate time comes, as if a light had suddenly illuminated their scene. The music used in the exercises links the story.

DEVELOPMENT OF PART OF THE STORY FOR CLASS IMPROVISATION, WITH THE TEACHER GUIDING AND SOMETIMES TAKING PART

Aims
1   to enable the children to think in depth about some problem relevant to the society in which they live.

2   to see the other point of view.

3   to make a group decision.

The Gypsy Encampment from Story No. 1
The class members decide on a problem that they, as gypsies, have to face. It is the threat of eviction from their site. They discuss their grievances, while the teacher questions their statements and puts forward the views of local residents. The gypsies retaliate by accusing the residents of prejudice. The teacher then puts forward some facts, ie, that property has been damaged and thefts reported. One of the gypsies admits the thefts, but gives reasons. The class then decide which of them will take the parts of the policeman and landowner. These two people come to the camp to question the gypsies and threaten them with eviction. Every so often the teacher acts as leader of one group or the other until a final settlement has been made and the problem to some degree solved.

The Native Village from Story No. 2
The villagers have a problem, because the two men have violated their temple. They have never experienced this before and call upon their leader for advice. They are a peaceful tribe and do not agree with their leader's decision to kill the men, but are forced by tribal obedience to carry it out. The tribe discuss the problem, with the teacher pointing out certain facts.

> *eg*   Might not the gods be angry if they kill them? If they do not kill them, the gods might be offended because their temple was violated. Should they follow the advice of the leader, if they feel it to be wrong?

They eventually make a decision having questioned the men and their motives and having consulted their leader. These examples stemmed from the creativity of a particular group. The problems they devised were their own. For the aims of these particular examples it is important that each group should be allowed to think for themselves and should not have the ideas of another group imposed upon them.

THE DEVELOPMENT OF IDEAS INTO A PLAY WITH GROUP CASTING
(12 to 13 year olds)

At this age, the ideas game becomes difficult because the boys are still immature and enjoy fights and adventure stories, while the girls are more sophisticated and concerned with clothes and romance. They still prefer to work apart, but the more mature ones of either sex will volunteer to work together; and when a group has worked together for some time, this co-operation spreads.

Combining the needs of both groups, we created a story which took place at the time of the French Revolution. It so happened that they were also covering this period in the history lesson.

Aims
1   To create a story.
2   To contrast controlled movement (soldiers) with apparently uncontrolled movement (mob); and give the shy children of this group, confidence to work together by using a background of music or sound effect.
3   To view execution from many points of view.
4   To construct the ideas into a short dramatic episode containing: groups of characters with leaders; a crowd scene with a climax of movement and sound, but in a controlled situation.

The Story
An important prisoner had been taken from the Bastille on his way to the guillotine. A great crowd was assembled to watch, consisting of generals and their wives, the rabble, always present at such events, and many soldiers. Unbeknown to the prisoner, plans had been made to help him escape. These plans were: to cause a disturbance in the crowd; pretend the Bastille was on fire and create a diversion among the elegant ladies, with a basket full of rats. The priest was also a rescuer in disguise and so at the crucial moment, the prisoner was freed, given a sword, and the five of them fought their way to safety crying '*Vive La France!*'

The Planning
1   The class becomes the rabble on its way to the execution. (Music...*Divertissement*...Finale by Ibert.)
2   Every member of the class becomes the Prisoner on his way to the guillotine, walking to a series of drum beats...he walks, climbs the stair, kneels, then bows his head.
3   The generals and their wives prepare themselves in front of a mirror and when ready process along the highway. (Music for

procession *Trumpet Fanfare.*)
4   In pairs. Controlled fights with swords to six counts of the drum beat, then ten and then in their own time.
5   In pairs. Two soldiers discuss the forthcoming execution and let their attitudes towards their job be known to each other.
6   In fours. The friends decide how to help the prisoner escape. (With the class concerned the groups chose their own methods, the whole class then discussed all the ideas. and arrived at the ones mentioned in the story above.)
7   In pairs. Two old people looking forward to the execution.
8   The block is built from rostra.
9   The groups are cast and the individual characters chosen by the teacher.
10   The end of the story is then tried with the fight and general panic of the people.
11   The first run through of the whole story using the same music to link the events, but encouraging as much speech as possible.
12   Discussion and second run through for quality.

SMALL GROUPS CREATING OWN SCENES STIMULATED BY FILM
SLIDES, PAINTINGS; PHOTOGRAPHS; SOUNDS; MUSIC OR OBJECTS

The excitement and enthusiasm of small group activity can often lead to squabbles over equipment and one group disturbing another. Therefore, it is often advisable to see that each group has planned whatever they need before they begin and that they are not monopolising all the rostra. A rule should be made that a group can only use an area belonging to someone else if there is no one there at that time. Although groups should be flowing and creative in their use of the hall, a mad chase of one group through a quiet sitting-room scene of another, can disrupt the whole lesson.

Very little can be stated in this section apart from the organisation, as it is purely creative and results are never the same. Some teachers may have already had experience of working on improvisation with small groups and so have started at this stage. Results can be quite good, but more often than not, only one or two small groups shine. If the children have had the opportunity to work on activities shown earlier in the progression, all the groups would be able to make a worthwhile contribution towards ideas, movement and speech. They need to be aware of the shape of their story. For example, that it has a good beginning, a climax and a definite ending with a decisive last line or event.

Visual Stimulus

Sometimes a group will prefer to work, first as individuals creating their own impressions, and gradually making their creation work with the others in the group. For example, the class may sit close to a slide thrown on to a cyclorama from a wide angled lens. Ideas are prolific and quite individual. They then return to their groups and together play out their ideas. The slide may have been abstract in form and the children might represent this abstraction, giving it a fluency which changes in shape upon meeting a similar one. This may involve movement only, or it could also involve sounds.

When viewing a strange painting or photograph, some groups prefer to discuss their ideas and make a communal decision. Then they plan their scene, decide on the situation and try out their ideas as a team.

Strange objects and items of costume, such as lengths of material or masks, can stimulate the imagination of the most inexperienced group.

Aural Stimulus

Small groups enjoy creating sounds. Drums can be made from old tins and old inner tubes. Pins or marbles in a tin; bottles with different levels of water, metallic noises and whistles of various descriptions are just a few possibilities. Electronic effects can be made by experimenting with a tape recorder. Older boys especially, would appreciate the music of John Cage and Edgar Varese who both experiment with sound.

Groups need to listen to the music once or twice before trying out their ideas. Finally they should listen in even greater detail so that they are able to harmonise their efforts. They become aware, not only of the mood, but of the opportunities created to synchronise phrase of music with phrase of movement, intensity with intensity, relaxation with relaxation.

There is a list at the back of the book which gives details of suitable music (page 138).

LEGENDS AND MYTHS

There are many legends and myths suitable for dramatisation and the members of the class will eventually reach the stage where they no longer need to split the story into activities, but will organise their ideas and co-operate one with another. They will need the teacher more for co-ordinator and sound technician than leader.

The Story   Persephone and King Pluto (10 year olds)

Persephone was the daughter of Ceres, Goddess of corn. She was a beautiful girl who spent many hours playing with her friends in the fields of flowers. King Pluto fell in love with her and was determined to have her. One day, while she was playing with her maidens, he came up from the ground in his chariot and carried her off. She refused to eat or drink and pined to return. Ceres, in desperation, swore that the earth should suffer perpetual winter unless her daughter was returned, and appealed to Zeus. Zeus promised her she might have her daughter back, if Persephone had not eaten any food in the Underworld. At the same time he ordered King Pluto to allow the girl to return home, and sent his messenger, Hermes, to fetch her. Pluto knew he could not keep Persephone unless she ate some of his food and he had been unable to persuade her. However, as she was about to leave with Hermes, one of Pluto's gardeners held up a broken pomegranate and said that he saw Persephone eat three seeds from the fruit. So Persephone had to stay with Pluto as his Queen for three months of the year, but she was allowed to return to her mother and the earth above for the remaining nine months. During these months, Ceres looked after all that grew in the earth. She touched the corn and it grew, turned yellow and ripened and she laid her hands on the trees and they blossomed and in time their branches hung low with fruit. But for the three months Persephone was away, nothing grew. It was winter. But the men and animals *did* not despair, for they knew Persephone would come back and that for nine months all would be well again and they called these nine months Spring, Summer and Autumn.

How the children planned the story

They decided who was to be Ceres, Persephone, Pluto, Hermes, Zeus and the old gardener. Some of them chose to be Pluto's servants, the girls to be Persephone's friends. They built a throne and a coach, decided upon the area for the field, Zeus' palace and the gateway to the Underworld.

They asked for music to accompany the play in the fields, and the four seasons, which they wanted to represent at the end. They also wanted some percussion, such as a drum or cymbal, for Pluto's sudden appearance and Hermes' flight.

They then gathered together and listed the order of the scenes which would flow from one to the other, linked with sound.

1   Ceres leaves her daughter and friends in the fields while she sows the corn. Then Pluto arrives and carries her off. The friends run to tell Ceres. There is a dance of despair.

2   Pluto's palace in the Underworld. He tries to persuade Persephone to be happy, eat and drink with him. She pleads to return.

3   Ceres calls upon Zeus to ask his advice. He gives it and orders Hermes to go to the Underworld.

4   Hermes does so and Pluto is reluctantly about to let Persephone return, when the old gardener tells what he has seen. Pluto is delighted and sends a message back with Hermes that Persephone will remain for three months.

5   Pluto and his servants now prepare for the wedding as a dance drama, the boys triumphant and Persephone still wishing to return to earth.

6   The girls dance, showing Spring changing to Summer and finally to Autumn.

APPROACHES TO THE SCRIPTED SCENE

In an unstreamed class there are some children who are ready to tackle a script, while others can barely read it and are immediately frightened by lack of understanding. The approaches described here give opportunity for both groups to experience success and extend those with lesser academic ability, giving them confidence to tackle the printed word.

MACBETH—ACT IV—SCENE I
(The Three Witches)

FIRST WITCH   Round about the cauldron go;
        In the poisoned entrails throw;
        Toad, that under cold stone
        Days and nights has thirty-one
        Swelter'd venom sleeping got,
        Boil thou first i' the charmed pot.
ALL   Double, double, toil and trouble;
        Fire burn and cauldron bubble.
SECOND WITCH   Fillet of a fenny snake,
        In the cauldron boil and bake;
        Eye of newt and toe of frog,
        Wool of bat, and tongue of dog;
        Adder's fork, and blind-worm's sting,
        Lizard's leg and howlet's wing;
        For a charm of powerful trouble,
        Like a hell broth, boil and bubble.
ALL   Double, double, toil and trouble,
        Fire burn and cauldron bubble.
THIRD WITCH   Scale of dragon, tooth of wolf,
        Witch's mummy, maw and gulf
        Of the ravin's salt sea shark;
        Root of hemlock digge'd i' the dark;
        Liver of blaspheming Jew,
        Gall of goat and slips of yew,
        Silver'd in the moon's eclipse;
        Nose of Turk and Tartar's lips;
        Finger of birth strangled babe,
        Ditch delivered by a drab
        Make the gruel thick and slab;
        Add thereto a tiger's chaudron,
        For the ingredients of our cauldron.
ALL   Double, double, toil and trouble;
        Fire burn and cauldron bubble.
SECOND WITCH   Cool it with a baboon's blood,
        Then the charm is firm and good.

The Planning

1   The members of the class listen to a short passage from
Stravinsky's *Rite of Spring*. They are asked to imagine a witch's
den in which there are shelves filled by strangely shaped bottles
and objects.

2   Accompanied by the music, the children, working simultaneously but as individuals, enter the den they have discovered and
examine the bottles and their contents.

3   In groups of three, they are asked to gather round a cauldron
and think of things they might throw into it. As each one
approaches the cauldron, they speak the name of the object and
hold their position for a second or two, as if mentally casting a
spell.

4   This is explored further and they are asked to change their
movement. For example, one approaching the cauldron in a curl-
ing manner, while another leaps towards it, the third crawling.
The ideas must spring from the children. They are asked to be
aware of the possibility of dramatic effect from the changing use
of levels, in the actual casting of the spell. For example, the first
would take a high level, while the second, seeing this, would take
a contrasting one and so on. Having experimented with this, the
groups show to each other and constructive criticism is possible.

5   Having worked on the movement, they now try to experiment
with the sounds and words they have chosen to say. Holding on
to sibilant or continuant sounds and spitting out plosives, while
attempting to harmonise the sound with their movement.

6   The refrain...'Double, double toil and trouble' is now committed to memory and the groups discuss three contrasting styles
of voice and movement, for when they have to repeat it three
times.

7   Now they are presented with copies of the script. They cast
themselves within their groups. The teacher helps them to understand the meaning of the words and they try it in their groups.
(Here the quality of movement and sound obtained shortly before,
is lost for a time, while they handle the sheet of paper and
struggle for the meaning.)

8   After the final attempt in small groups, comes the sharing
with each other by those who want to show their work. (Now the
quality begins to return and if the words are committed to
memory, the movement and expressive use of sounds make the

scene meaningful to all concerned.)

UNDER MILK WOOD—DYLAN THOMAS

In the following episodes, the words are simple to understand, have an easy rhythm which is a joy to speak and repetition of the scenes allows those of lesser ability to remember and so aid their reading. The themes appeal to the adolescent, the characters being clearly drawn and the dialogue dramatic. Here the script can be approached without improvisation, it would have little value in the approach of this text.

In each scene, the children could discuss either as a class or in groups, the type of person which the lines reflect; how such a person would dress, move and speak. After this generalisation, can be added the creative touches which make the characters personal to the interpreters.

So often, when given a script, the natural rhythms of speech disappear, even when it has been learned by heart. It is always obvious when the cast of a school play have been given the script to learn on their own, before rehearsals have started. It creates an almost impossible task for the producer, because once the lines have been learned in a certain way, it is extremely difficult to get a child to change them.

Some scenes, like the 'Ogmore-Pritchards' have a poetic quality and some of the lines demand an equal pause at the end. Normal speech rhythms however, do not have this equal pause between one person speaking and the next, or at commas and full stops. Some people are able to sense this with ease, while others find it extremely difficult.

The Kissing Game needs plenty of movement, the sing song rhythm of children's games and a good climax of speed and sound at the end.

The last scene with Mr and Mrs Pugh enables the children playing the parts to portray thoughts, read by the narrator, with a flicker of a smile or a raised eyebrow.

UNDER MILK WOOD

Mrs Ogmore-Pritchard, Mr Ogmore and Mr Pritchard

MRS OGMORE-PRITCHARD Mr Ogmore!
Mr Pritchard!
It is time to inhale your balsam.
MR OGMORE Oh, Mrs Ogmore!
MR PRITCHARD Oh, Mrs Pritchard!
MRS OGMORE-PRITCHARD Soon it will be time to get up.
Tell me your tasks, in order.
MR OGMORE I must put my pyjamas in the drawer marked
'pyjamas'.
MR PRITCHARD I must take my cold bath which is good for me.
MR OGMORE I must wear my flannel band to ward off sciatica.
MR PRITCHARD I must dress behind the curtain and put on my
apron.
MR OGMORE I must blow my nose.
MRS OGMORE-PRITCHARD In the garden, if you please.
MR OGMORE In a piece of tissue-paper which I afterwards burn.
MR PRITCHARD I must take my salts which are nature's friend.
MR OGMORE I must boil the drinking water because of germs.
MR PRITCHARD I must make my herb tea which is free from
tannin.
MR OGMORE And have a charcoal biscuit which is good for me.
MR PRITCHARD I may smoke one pipe of asthma mixture.
MRS OGMORE-PRITCHARD In the woodshed, if you please.
MR PRITCHARD And dust the parlour and spray the canary.
MR OGMORE I must put on rubber gloves and search the peke
for fleas.
MR PRITCHARD I must dust the blinds and then I must raise
them.
MRS OGMORE-PRITCHARD And before you let the sun in, mind it
wipes its shoes.

Lily Smalls and the Beynons

LILY SMALLS   Oh, there's a face!
    Where you get that hair from?
    Got it from a old tom cat.
    Give it back then, love.
    Oh there's a perm!

    Where you get that nose from, Lily?
    Got it from my father, silly.
    You've got it on upside down!
    Oh there's a conk!
    Look at your complexion!
    Oh no, you look.
    Needs a bit of make-up.
    Needs a veil.
    Oh there's glamour!

    Where you get that smile, Lil?
    Never you mind, girl.
    Nobody loves you.
    That's what you think.
    Who is it loves you?
    Shan't tell.
    Come on, Lily.
    Cross your heart, then?
    Cross my heart.
FIRST VOICE   And very softly, her lips almost touching her
reflection, she breathes the name and clouds the shaving-glass.
MRS BEYNON   *(Loudly, from above)* Lily!
LILY SMALLS   *(Loudly)*   Yes, mum.
MRS BEYNON   Where's my tea, girl?
LILY SMALLS   *(Softly)* Where d'you think? In the cat-box?
(Loudly) Coming up, mum.

Mr and Mrs Cherry Owen

MRS CHERRY OWEN   See that smudge on the wall by the picture
of Auntie Blossom?
      That's where you threw the sago.

(Cherry Owen laughs with delight)

CHERRY OWEN   I always miss Auntie Blossom too.
      You only missed me by an inch.
MRS CHERRY OWEN   Remember last night? In you reeled, my
      boy, as drunk as a deacon with a big wet bucket and a fish-
      frail full of stout and you looked at me and you said, ' God
      has come home!' you said, and then over the bucket you
      went, sprawling and bawling, and the floor was all flagons
      and eels.
CHERRY OWEN   Was I wounded?
MRS CHERRY OWEN   And then you took off your trousers and
      you said, ' Does anybody want a fight!' Oh, you old baboon.
CHERRY OWEN   Give me a kiss.
MRS CHERRY OWEN   And then you sang 'Bread of Heaven',
      tenor and bass.
CHERRY OWEN   I always sing 'Bread of Heaven'.
MRS CHERRY OWEN   And then you did a little dance on the table.
CHERY OWEN   I did?
MRS CHERRY OWEN   Drop dead!
CHERRY OWEN   And then what did I do?
MRS CHERRY OWEN   Then you cried like a baby and said you
      were a poor drunk orphan with nowhere to go but the grave.
CHERRY OWEN   And what did I do next, my dear?
MRS CHERRY OWEN   Then you danced on the table all over again
      and said you were King Solomon Owen and I was your Mrs
      Sheba.
CHERRY OWEN   *(Softly)* And then?
MRS CHERRY OWEN   And then I got you into bed and you snored
      all night like a brewery.

Lily Smalls and the Beynons

MRS BEYNON   She likes the liver, Ben.
MR BEYNON   She ought to do, Bess. It's her brother's.
MRS BEYNON   *(Screaming)* Oh, d'you hear that, Lily?
LILY SMALLS   Yes, mum.
MRS BEYNON   We're eating pusscat.
LILY SMALLS   Yes, mum.
MRS BEYNON   Oh, you cat-butcher!
MR BEYNON   It was doctored, mind.
MRS BEYNON   *(Hysterical)* What's that got to do with it?
MR BEYNON   Yesterday we had mole.
MRS BEYNON   Oh, Lily, Lily!
MR BEYNON   Monday, otter. Tuesday, shrews.

(Mrs Beynon screams)

LILY SMALLS   Go on, Mrs Beynon. He's the biggest liar in town.
MRS BEYNON   Don't you dare say that about Mr Beynon.
LILY SMALLS   Everybody knows it, mum.
MRS BEYNON   Mr Beynon never tells a lie. Do you, Ben?
MR BEYNON   No, Bess. And now I am going out after the corgies with my little cleaver.
MRS BEYNON   Oh, Lily, Lily!

Mrs Dai Bread One and Mrs Dai Bread Two

MRS DAI BREAD TWO   Cross my palm with silver. Out of our housekeeping money. Aah!
MRS DAI BREAD ONE   What d'you see, lovie?
MRS DAI BREAD TWO   I see a featherbed. With three pillows on it. And a text above the bed. I can't read what it says, there's great clouds blowing. Now they have blown away. God is Love, the text says.
MRS DAI BREAD ONE   *(Delighted)* That's our bed.
MRS DAI BREAD TWO   And now it's vanished. The sun's spinning like a top. Who's this coming out of the sun? It's a hairy little man with big pink lips. He's got a wall eye.

MRS DAI BREAD ONE   It's Dai, it's Dai Bread!

MRS DAI BREAD TWO   Ssh! The featherbed's floating back. The little man's taking his boots off. He's pulling his shirt over his head. He's beating his chest with his fists. He's climbing into bed.

MRS DAI BREAD ONE   Go on, go on.

MRS DAI BREAD TWO   There's two women in bed. He looks at them both, with his head cocked on one side. He's whistling through his teeth. Now he grips his little arms round one of the women.

MRS DAI BREAD ONE   Which one, which one?

MRS DAI BREAD TWO   I can't see any more. There's great clouds blowing again.

MRS DAI BREAD ONE   Ach, the mean old clouds!

The boys and the girl's kissing game

GIRLS' VOICES   Gwennie call the boys
They make such a noise.

GIRL   Boys boys boys
Come along to me.

GIRLS' VOICES   Boys boys boys
Kiss Gwennie where she says
Or give her a penny
Go on, Gwennie.

GIRL   Kiss me in Goosegog Lane
Or give me a penny.
What's your name?

FIRST BOY   Billy.

GIRL   Kiss me in Goosegog Lane Billy
Or give me a penny silly.

FIRST BOY   Gwennie Gwennie
I kiss you in Goosegog Lane.
Now I haven't got to give you a penny.

GIRLS' VOICES   Boys boys boys
Kiss Gwennie where she says
Or give her a penny.
Go on, Gwennie.

GIRL   Kiss me on Llaregyb Hill
      Or give me a penny.
      What's your name?
SECOND BOY   Johnnie Cristo.
GIRL   Kiss me on Llaregyb Hill Johnnie Cristo
      Or give me a penny mister.
SECOND BOY   Gwennie Gwennie
      I kiss you on Llaregyb Hill.
      Now I haven't got to give you a penny.
GIRLS' VOICES   Boys boys boys
      Kiss Gwennie where she says
      Or give her a penny.
      Go on, Gwennie.
GIRL   Kiss me in Milk Wood
      Or give me a penny.
      What's your name?
THIRD BOY   Dicky.
GIRL   Kiss me in Milk Wood Dicky
      Or give me a penny quickly.
THIRD BOY   Gwennie Gwennie
      I can't kiss you in Milk Wood.
GIRLS' VOICES   Gwennie ask him why.
GIRL   Why?
THIRD BOY   Because my mother says I mustn't.
GIRLS' VOICES   Cowardy cowardy custard.
      Give Gwennie a penny.
GIRL   Give me a penny.
THIRD BOY   I haven't got any.
GIRLS' VOICES   Put him in the river
      Up to his liver
      Quick quick Dirty Dick
      Beat him on the bum
      With a rhubarb stick.
      Aiee!
      Hush!

Mr and Mrs Pugh

MRS PUGH   Persons with manners do not read at table.

FIRST VOICE   says Mrs Pugh. She swallows a digestive tablet as big as a horse-pill, washing it down with clouded peasoup water.

(Pause)

MRS PUGH   Some persons were brought up in pigsties.

MR PUGH   Pigs don't read at table, dear.

FIRST VOICE   Bitterly she flicks dust from the broken cruet. It settles on the pie in a thin gnat-rain.

MR PUGH   Pigs can't read, my dear.

MRS PUGH   I know one who can.

FIRST VOICE   Alone in the hissing laboratory of his wishes, Mr Pugh minces among bad vats and jeroboams, tiptoes through spinneys of murdering herbs, agony dancing in his crucibles, and mixes especially for Mrs Pugh a venomous porridge unknown to toxicologists which will scald and viper through her until her ears fall off like figs, her toes grow big and black as balloons, and steam comes screaming out of her navel.

MR PUGH   You know best, dear.

FIRST VOICE   Says, Mr Pugh, and quick as a flash he ducks her in rat soup.

MRS PUGH   What's that book by your trough, Mr Pugh?

MR PUGH   It's a theological work, my dear. Lives of the Great Saints.

FIRST VOICE   Mrs Pugh smiles. An icicle forms in the cold air of the dining-vault.

CORIOLANUS

This play is not a popular one in schools, but the last scene affords scope for improvisation within a crowd scene, leading to a climax of sound and movement. The leading characters are powerful and the scene contains three changes of mood. It could be presented as part of a study of the play or as an exercise in itself. An exciting scene like this can introduce a play to a class. A theme such as 'Shakespeare's Assassinations' could introduce many characters and give them a 'feeling' for the style of language.

The Story

Caius Marcius was a Roman soldier and the Romans were at war with the Volscians who lived in Corioli. The poor people of Rome disliked Caius Marcius because he was proud and being an important nobleman held power in the city. The poor were starving because of the money being spent on wars.

Tullus Aufidius left the city of Corioli with an army and while he was away, Marcius took a Roman army and fought Corioli. The Romans were being defeated and had had to retreat, when Marcius suddenly followed the Volscian soldiers back into their city and the gates shut behind him leaving him alone to fight. This spurred the Roman soldiers to return and climb the walls to help him. Between them they conquered the city and went back to Rome triumphant. They re-named him Coriolanus. Aufidius, hearing of the victory stayed at a town called Antium. The other nobleman of Rome, now wanted to make Coriolanus a Consul, but he annoyed the people by mocking them during a ritual when he was meant to be humble; and his enemies incited the crowd to kill him. He was very annoyed and made some rude remarks about the Romans running away from the battle. Then all turned against him. He was sentenced to banishment. He left his wife, son and mother behind and went to seek Aufidius in Antium.

He knew Aufidius because he had often fought with him, but never beaten him. When he offered his services to the Volscians, Aufidius pretended to be grateful and they both returned to Corioli and took over the city. Every battle they fought, Coriolanus won for them. Eventually the wars took them to the gates of Rome. This was all Aufidius had been waiting for. When they had conquered Rome, he planned to kill Coriolanus, However, outside Rome, Coriolanus' wife, little son and mother came and pleaded with him to make peace with his own people. Eventually and in front of Aufidius, he agreed to do so.

On returning to Corioli, Aufidius plots with the conspirators and they succeed in arousing the crowd to kill Coriolanus. At the end however, Aufidius is reminded of his noble and brave character and shows remorse that such a man had to die.

The Planning

1 The story is told to the class and not necessarily presented as Shakespeare. (As the story is rather complicated, large Flash cards indicating the three countries, Antium, Corioli and Rome can be held by members of the class, while the other characters with similar cards enact the journeys from one country to another.)

2 Rostra are set out as a raised area of a market place with steps around the sides.

3 With the teacher as the centre piece, the class becomes the angry crowd and approaches the rostrum with the chant 'Kill him, kill him, kill, kill, kill, kill' and work towards timing the climax of sound with the movement and freezing after the climax. (With most groups this will take some time to perfect, but it is worth the effort, because it demands self-control and concentration from the whole group. There is always one child who feels compelled to say 'Kill him' when everyone else has stopped!)

4 In pairs—Aufidius and Coriolanus discuss and finally argue as to why Coriolanus made peace. The final insult comes when Aufidius refers to him as a boy. This infuriates Coriolanus who then reminds him of the time he entered the gates and fought them all single handed.

5 In fours—Three friends of Aufidius try to persuade him to get rid of Coriolanus. They remind him how he, Aufidius entered the city unacclaimed, while they can hear the cheers given to Coriolanus, by countrymen whose relations he once slew.

6 Processional music and fanfares. A 'Coriolanus' is chosen and the class, using as much space as is available follows him round the hall, cheering and acclaiming him as if they were a mob of peasants.

7 This is then recorded on tape to be used later.

8 The script of the final scene is now given out (a slightly cut version) and the teacher reads it to them.

9 Aufidius and Coriolanus are cast and the middle section read

to ensure that the correct emphasis comes with understanding of the mood and situation, while the rest rehearse the climax of sound at the murder.

10 The Lords and Conspirators are cast and the scene then acted out in the hall area, the tape recording of the crowd giving a realistic backing to the actual crowd noises made by the rest of the class.

11 Discussion about the reactions of the crowd. (The final production of the scene would vary with each teacher, but the crowd scene will need more thought if it is to be convincing. The crowd will realise that they are experiencing five different emotions; jubilation, doubt, suspicion, anger and fury. Discussion on personal reactions to these emotions regarding timing and character will help to make the class realise that the crowd are real people, important to the scene and not just extras saying 'Rhubarb, rhubarb, rhubarb'.)

12 Practice of the last section, the falling of Coriolanus down the steps, the carrying of the body away from the area, the declimax, etc.

13 The final polishing with sound effects of crowd, fanfare and drum beat. (If the scene is enacted on a stage and lighting is available, the lighting change can help convey the change of mood.)

CORIOLANUS—ACT V—SCENE VI

Drums and sounds of great shouts from the people
Aufidius waits with three conspirators

AUFIDIUS Hark!
FIRST CONSPIRATOR Your native town you entered like a post,
 And has no welcomes home; but he returns,
 Splitting the air with noise.
SECOND CONSPIRATOR And patient fools,
 Whose children he hath slain, their base throats tear
 With giving him glory.
THIRD CONSPIRATOR Therefore, at your vantage
 Ere he express himself, or move the people

With what he would say, let him feel your sword,
Which we will second.

AUFIDIUS   Say no more.

Enter the LORDS *of the city*

LORDS   You are most welcome home.

AUFIDIUS   I have not deserved it.
But wealthy Lords, have you with heed perused
What I have written to you?

LORDS   We have.

FIRST LORD   And grieve to hear it.

AUFIDIUS   He approaches: you shall hear him.

Enter CORIOLANUS *with fanfare and* CROWD *cheering*

CORIOLANUS   Hail Lords! I am returned your soldier:
You are to know,
That properously I have attempted, and,
With bloody passage, led your wars even to
The gates of Rome. Our spoils we have brought home
We have made peace with no less honour to the Antiates
Than shame to the Romans; and we here deliver
What we have compounded on.

AUFIDIUS   Read it not, noble lords;
But tell the traitor, in the highest degree
He hath abused your powers.

CORIOLANUS   Traitor! How now!

AUFIDIUS   Ay, Traitor, Marcius.

CORIOLANUS   Marcius?

AUDIFIUS   Ay, Marcius. Caius Marcius: dost thou think
I'll grace thee with that stolen name
Coriolanus, in Corioli—?
You lords and heads of the state, perfidiously
He has betrayed your business, and given up,
For certain drops of salt, your city, Rome—
I say *your* city—to his wife and mother,
Breaking his oath and resolution, like
A twist of rotten silk.
Thou boy of tears.

FIRST LORD   Peace both and hear me speak.

CORIOLANUS   Boy!
Cut me to pieces Volsces, men and lads.

Stain all your edges on me. Boy! False hound.
If you have writ your annals true, 'tis there
That, like an eagle in a dovecoate, I
Fluttered your Volscians in Corioli:
Alone I did it. Boy!

AUFIDIUS Why, noble lords,
Will you be put in mind of his blind fortune,
Which was your shame, by this unholy braggart,
'Fore your own eyes and ears? Insolent Villian.

CROWD Let him die for it.
Tear him to pieces—Do it presently—
He killed my son—he killed my daughter—
Marcius—etc.
Kill, kill, kill kill, kill him!

They all fall upon him (as the following say):

LORDS Hold, hold, hold.

AUFIDIUS My noble masters, hear me speak.

Coriolanus falls dead

SECOND LORD O Tullus! Thou has done a deed whereat valour
will weep.

THIRD LORD Tread not upon him—Masters, all, be quiet.
Put up your swords.

FIRST LORD Bear from hence his body—
And mourn you for him; let him be regarded
As the most noble corpse that ever herald
Did follow to his urn.

AUFIDIUS My rage is gone;
And I am struck with sorrow. Take him up.
Help five of the chiefest soldiers; I'll be one—
Beat thou the drum, that it speak mournfully;
Trail your steel pikes. Though in this city he
Hath widowed and unchilded many a one,
Which to this hour bewail the injury,
Yet he shall have a noble memory—
Assist.

They exit bearing the body while the drum sounds.

THE SCHOOL PLAY AT 14 PLUS

It is generally accepted that the school play should provide an opportunity for many to take part and not be for the privileged few. Modern thinking in educational drama has made people aware of this, yet at the same time has given some teachers the impression that the school play is not necessary. It is an unfortunate impression because theatre is a natural part of any civilised society. It is the adult expression of play. There are those who prefer to act; others who prefer to watch. The team work involved in a school play is a very natural happening for a community and can be a most worthwhile one. Great enjoyment is usually had by all, despite the anxieties of rehearsals and casting. Many departments come together to work on the project and the children concerned experience co-operation not only among themselves, but among adults who work with them. Working relationships are sometimes experienced which are difficult to obtain in a classroom situation and very often it encourages parents to help. Many parents would never visit the school but for the school play.

This special occasion in the school year should provide a workshop for creative arts, which embraces the art of taping music and sound effects: artistic lighting which expresses the mood or directs the eye; designing and painting both costumes and scenery; movement and speech. The producer should head a team working with his actor's ideas and limitations, moulding to an overall shape which appeals to ear and eye. The producer selects the final shape, but the actor will gain more satisfaction from having been able to create for himself or within the group, rather than being pushed about like a puppet.

A teacher who has used music, movement and the children's own imaginative powers in the school drama period, will not be satisfied with the ordinary play which simply presents a story in an average set with unchallenging characters...and this presents a problem. In a school of mixed ability, with the top age range only 14 or 15, the classics present an experience for a few, an experience of which they should not be deprived, but for the majority the result would be the stereotyped impression one has of the school play—static, wordy and unrealistic. In other words, too difficult for the abilities of most of the children concerned. However, average children have great capabilities, if given the right material and opportunities to develop their potential. They have an enormous amount of energy and enthusiasm to contribute, if the theme appeals.

The following comments give some indication of the range of dramatic productions now taking place in schools, and may present some new ideas to those seeking suitable material. The harmony of lighting, sound and movement is the key to the success of these productions and I have sometimes taken the opportunity to describe the lighting/sound effects in detail.

The Business of Good Government by John Arden (Methuen)
This is a Christmas play which allows for a flexible production. It can be adapted to suit any shape of hall or stage. The scenes flow from one to the other linked by music or songs. The language is a mixture of down to earth speech and poetry. There is comedy, fear, beauty and wonder. There is the atmosphere of the court, the miracle and the hillside. There is opportunity for a dance drama in the Massacre of the Innocents and for the beauty of a solo voice singing unaccompanied. Acting areas are lit only when necessary and characters remain in view moving from their places when it is time for their scene. Processions or journeys can take place through the audience and so give a greater impression of space and time.

The Boy with a Cart by Christopher Fry (Muller)
This is another religious play, with language which proves easy for the villagers, comic characters and mowers. Cuthman's long speeches flow easily but, to be fully convincing, need understanding on the part of the young actor. Here again, the play provides comedy alongside wonder. There are crowd scenes which allow for improvisation within the script; and the Rain chorus, which is one of the highlights of the play, is ideal for choral speaking and movement to words.

Avenue arena (with the audience facing each other, stage at one end used as entrance to the church) is a very good method of staging, as the journey with the cart takes up a lot of room and a number of entrances are desired to give the logical positions of village, etc. 'In the round', can also be used effectively, but the 'proscenium' has limitations.

Example of lighting effect at the end of the play The villagers are assembled on the floor of the hall, disheartened because they cannot get the king post into place and fear the church will never be finished. Cuthman then appears on the apron in front of the stage curtains, walking slowly; they notice him, he speaks and tells them that the church will be finished. As he begins to speak, a spotlight comes up on him, very slowly. At the same time, the lights on the floor area, fade. This is called a cross fade. As he tells of the miracle, so the intensity of the light is increased and music is brought in softly under his words. When he reaches the lines....

> There under the bare walls of our labour,
> Life and death were knitted in one strength....

the stage curtains open a little to reveal a wooden cross hung from the centre of the stage. A light behind this cross now cross fades with the one on Cuthman, throwing him into silhouette. This happens very slowly as he turns and walks towards the cross on the line...

> Indivisible as root and sky.

As Cuthman raises the volume of his voice, so the volume of the music rises and the light again grows in intensity. The villagers begin to follow him silently and as the music reaches the climax and the last villager has entered the church, the light fades and the curtains close. The music used was the end of the *Great Gate of Kiev* from *Pictures at an Exhibition* by Mussorgsky.

It Should Happen to a Dog by Wolf Mankowitz, Five One Act Plays (Evans)
This play consists of a bare outline of a number of scenes with a minimum of dialogue. It presents a challenge to the producer's imagination and the playwright encourages the producer to be imaginative. It tells the story of Jonah and the Whale and makes an ideal vehicle for an enthusiastic group to express their feelings about the world today. It is a strange mixture of past and present and so permits anachronisms. Nineveh, for example, can depict the present and could contain a dance drama and improvisation similar to the following:
1   The King seated in his harem watching television, a tape having been made which satirises advertising, the press, religion,

sex, and hire-purchase, etc.

2 A stylised Bingo session, working towards a climax of 'House'.

3 A comic drug pedlar selling his wares, followed by a dance drama showing the influence of drugs upon the body, voice and mind. The dance could incorporate a 'Pop' session, a gang fight showing colour prejudice and ending by the group turning upon Jonah who tries to intervene.

Similarly, the mood can be symbolised in movement and music, when they are waiting for the last few days to pass. When they realise the forty days are over, the rejoicing begin and they return to their old ways.

The ship and market scenes lend themselves to musical improvisation before the commencement of the dialogue. *Bach before the Mast* is ideal music for the entrance of the sailors, while Ted Heath's *Shish Kebab* is excellent for the market scene which opens the play.

Scenery could consist of a number of rostra re-arranged by the actors to change the market to a ship and later, to Nineveh. Then the actors can 'flow' on and off the stage as the rostra provide the link in heights. This intimate staging enables the actors to have closer contact with the audience and if desired entrances can be made from the back of the hall.

Acting areas can be lit as the players use them, so directing the glance of the audience on to the centre of attention. The scenes are then linked by lighting and sound, so that there are no unnecessary pauses and one scene flows into the next.

Falpelion (A modern Tempest)

This was a science fiction play written by the English staff of a Comprehensive school from improvisations with the children, on themes and situations from the story.

The first scene took place in a space ship and lasted a few minutes, giving the impression of the ship, a few minutes before it crashed onto an unknown planet. Scenery for such a short time was impractical, but rostra were already on the stage for the next scene and arranged at different levels, so the crew were arranged in a 'V' formation and lit only by torches held up to their faces and switched on one at a time synchronised with the music *Electronic Movements—Syncopation* by Tom Disseveldt.

Life was discovered on this planet. It consisted of a man, his daughter and her nurse. The creatures which served her were large insects; those who flew and were beautiful and those who were like beetles and came from the dark side of the planet.

Their adventures flowed from scene to scene. The production was a proscenium one and the use of the apron and side areas allowed time for simple scene changes, without disrupting the flow of the action. Again lighting and sound linked the scenes. The dark side of the planet was lit only with ultra-violet light and the actors' costumes, made and designed by the staff and children working in the needlework department, had white stripes, washed in a detergent containing a 'phosphorescing' agent, such as *Daz*. A solution of *Daz* and *Polycell* (or a paper-hanger's paste) enabled hands and faces to be seen in a strange mauve light. There were many good acrobats in the school and these boys were delighted to take part, performing the activity they enjoyed most. They were involved in the action on the dark side of the planet. From a trampoline off stage they leapt, tossed and tumbled to the music, creating a startling effect when only their costumes were lit and they appeared as if from nowhere, tumbling through the air.

The Dance Circle created a dance for the court scene and the music department provided some boys who were able to create strange sounds with percussion.

The result was a play which generated great enthusiasm among all departments and the children of lesser ability were able to make a big contribution towards its success.

The Gun   contributed by Anthony Halford

The script for *The Gun* was inspired by children. A play centred round the attempts of three boys to rule and discipline a group of children who had escaped the bomb. Children whose cardboard crooks always appeared so insincere, were filled with instinctive energy when confronted with a situation they recognised from their own experience. Violent attitudes were confronted with more pacific counterparts. Eventually the physically powerful leader won control. He had no need of the gun.

The story was complex in its detail, but the cast had worked around a framework, assimilated it and worked out a script. They used their own names and some identified completely becoming totally absorbed in the action. However, they realised it was a framework which had to be theatrically convincing and so followed the director's guidance.

The result was a fast moving play which flowed through the hall, from the floor to the apron with sincerity and dramatic teamwork that left you breathless. The language was brutal but clear and dynamic. It offended many in its reality but it was a stepping stone. Once the children had discovered they could project their own personalities, they were able to project themselves into other characters. As a matter of interest, their next production was *The Business of Good Government*. Here the high standard of acting, or their complete identity and sincerity was continued, Herod's own humiliation being very close to 'the Boy' in *The Gun* who had been deprived of power.

The Land of Golden Days   contributed by Raymond White
This play took a new look at the Pied Piper story. They examined more closely the responses and attitudes of people involved in the plague of rats, not forgetting the role of the children. They also tried to show the nature of the townsfolk, their habitual moral posturing, influenced the course of events and made inevitable the piper's 'revenge'. Their revelation of the piper's reaction differed materially from Browning's and perhaps indicated the need for Everyman to involve himself in his own destiny. Change is the essence of life, as it is of drama and the resistance to change is part of the universal conflict in which we are all protagonists. Parents, as well as civic leaders, were vested with power and responsibility and found they must exercise these according to their lights, but they had no special claims to wisdom, which indeed may be revealed in unexpected ways and in insignificant persons.

The piper, although his 'magic' was central to the plot, was no Prospero. He rather explained than directed; rather revealed than controlled. His concern for the people of the town was charismatic and in no way motivated by self-interest; this was his importance in the play.

This was a musical, with songs created by the music department. They attempted to make them something more than parenthetical asides by planning each one as the crystallisation of a mood or an explanation of a character. In this way they highlighted, rather than halted, the action of the play.

The spontaneity of the crowd scenes, the natural reaction, completely in character, to an unexpected remark or happening and the energy and enthusiasm emitted from the large cast was a joy to watch. They had something to say, they understood it and conveyed it and their enjoyment to the audience.

A VARIETY OF ACTIVITIES BASED ON A THEME FOR THE TERM (12 to 15 year olds)

Theme A Holiday in Spain.
Introduction materials Holiday posters and brochures; Spanish shawls, dolls, dresses, objects and records.
Lesson 1 Individual work to music...Packing.
Crowd scene work...The railway station.
Group casting...Story taking place in the station with three large groups—school children—passengers—station employees—
Ideas Game...Story theme ' Mistaken identity '.
Lesson 2 Polished version of the above story.
Lesson 3 Individual work to teacher's narration...Inside the train.
Small group work...Inside the train.
Lesson 4 Individual imaginative work with a background of music...Arrival at destination; first impressions of hotel and room, etc.
Improvisation in pairs...Establishing relationships with people; language difficulties, etc.
Lesson 5 Movement work to teacher's narration...The beach.
Crowd scene work...The beach.
Lesson 6 Small group work...The first sight seeing tour to a Spanish castle. Title *Suspicion*. Story to be serialised and continued during lessons 7 and 8.
Lesson 7 Imaginative movement to teacher's narration...The underground caves is the second tour.
Small group work...continued *Suspicion Confirmed*.
Lesson 8 Movement work to music, individually and in pairs...
The third tour is the Bull fight.
Crowd scene work...The Bull fight.
Small group work...continued *Things Come To a Head*.

Lesson 9 Ritual and Processional work. Movement and crowd scenes...The Festival...Religious procession and ceremony.

Lesson 10 Script work approached through improvisation... Holidaymakers used as extras in big film epic.

Lesson 11 Movement to teacher's narration The last morning on the beach.

Free interpretation of music...A dream sequence.

Lesson 12 Improvisation in pairs and small groups...The farewell and start of the journey home.

Discussion of the term's work.

FURTHER REFERENCE
An Introduction to Child Drama by Peter Slade, University of London Press.
Legend and Drama Books 1 and 2 by Philip Payne, Ginn.
Exploration Drama – Legend by William Martin and Gordon Vallins, Evans.
Stories for Improvisation in Primary and Secondary Schools by Peter Chilver, Batsford.
Acting Shakspeare by Bernard Joseph, Longmans.
Drama and Theatre in Education, H.E.B.

Drama and English

DRAMATIC POETRY

Some dramatic poetry lends itself to a tripartite expression of dance, music and words. The examples given here are *Jabberwocky*, *The Forsaken Merman*, *Drugged* and *The Ancient Mariner*. The whole poem is not always presented to the class. Instead they are given the story, the mood and a sample of the poetry. To do the poems justice, a hall is needed, with time to develop the story over a few weeks, the aim being a polished ' creation' at the end of that period.

Jabberwocky by Lewis Carroll (suitable for 9 to 11 year olds)
  'Twas brillig and the slithy toves
  Did gyre and gimble in the wabe;
  All mimsy were the borogroves,
  And the mome raths outgrabe.

  ' Beware the Jabberwock, my son
  The jaws that bite, the claws that catch !
  Beware the Jubjub bird, and shun
  The frumius Bandersnatch !'

  He took his vorpal sword in hand :
  Long time the manxome foe he sought—
  So rested he, by a Tumtum tree,
  And stood awhile in thought.

  And as in uffish thought he stood,
  The Jabberwock, with eyes of flame,
  Came whiffling through the tulgey wood
  And burbled as it came

One, two! One, two! And through and through
The vorpal blade went snicker-snack!
He left it dead, and with its head
He went galumphing back.

'And hast thou slain the Jabberwock?
Come to my arms, my beamish boy!
Oh frabjous day! Callooh! Callay!
He chortled in his joy.

'Twas brillig, and the slithy toves
Did gyre and gimble in the wabe;
All mimsy were the borogroves,
And the mome raths outgrabe.'

The Planning

1 The poem is introduced to the group. The whole poem could
be read, or just the names of the imaginary animals. Another
approach might be to show them some of the rubbery monsters
sold in toy shops. Then the class experiment with movement and
sounds to create the Slithy Toves, the Mome Raths, the Jubjub
bird, Borogroves and Jabberwocky. (The record *Jungle Noises,*
makes an interesting background if you do not want the class to
create its own effects.)
2 In pairs, Father and Son. They learn by repetition, the verse
spoken by the 'Father' and create for themselves his character
and dialect. They then change parts.
3 Individually, they all search the forest for the Jabberwock,
attack and kill him. (Opportunity to work on climax.)
4 A group may like to be narrators. If a microphone is available, the voices can then be heard over the music and it also
creates the eerie atmosphere. The members of the class then
choose to become one of the creatures and the hall becomes the
forest. The father and son are cast and the father might learn
and express the lines in his own way.
5 The polished version can be staged as a play, with lighting
effects and more movement, either on the stage or floor. Simple
masks and small properties can add to the interest and effect.

The Forsaken Merman by Matthew Arnold *(suitable for 9 to 12 year olds)*

For this particular example, the story is not told at the beginning

nor the poem discussed. Rostra are spaced informally on the
floor of the hall and chairs are available.

The Planning

1   Members of the class are asked to imagine that they live in a
fishing village about a hundred years ago. They can work in
pairs or small groups and decide what kind of occupation they
would be doing ('Sea effects' record is a suitable background for
this activity.)
2   Each child is asked to place a chair in a space quite a distance
away from him and then return to his original position. The first
exercise is then repeated, but this time ends with the church bell
ringing. (This can be done quite simply with two metal tubes.)
Each villager puts away his task and goes to sit in the church,
(the chair he placed previously), ready for the service.
3   They now work in pairs and label themselves A and B. Their
chairs should be placed a little away from each other, as if they
were in the same church. They listen to the final organ music
(*Jesu Joy of Man's Desiring* or other anthem) then slowly leave.
This is repeated, but now A is the person who has been away
from the village for quite a time. He or she disappeared one night
and no one knew where. Now A is sitting in the church and B
catches sight of A. As soon as they leave the service B rushes
up to ask where A has been. A makes up some excuse and hides
the truth.
4   They change over parts and try again. The members of the
class now share their 'excuses'.
5   They come and sit on the floor near the teacher and are told
the real reason, in fact the story of the poem.

The Story

Many years ago, Margaret left the fishing village to become the
wife of a Sea King. At first, she was very happy and they had
children who belonged to the sea, but she often felt homesick
for the land and felt remorse at losing her soul. So, one Easter
Day, when the church bells tolled down through the waves, she
persuaded her husband to let her return to the land to pray.
She promised she would return. However, she never kept her
promise and although she could hear her children calling her and
she felt sad at heart, she shut her window and refused to hear.

The Poem

The music of Ravel's *Daphnis and Chloe* accompanies the words. If it is possible to use a microphone, it ensures that all the class hear the description while still enjoying the full volume of the music. If not, the volume should be fairly low and the narrator should have the class close to him.

> Sand-strewn caverns, cool and deep,
> Where the winds are all asleep;
> Where the spent lights quiver and gleam;
> Where the salt weed sways in the stream;
> Where the sea-beasts rang'd all round
> Feed in the ooze of their pasture-ground;
> Where the sea-snakes coil and twine,
> Dry their mail and bask in the brine;
> Where great whales come sailing by,
> Sail and sail, with unshut eye,
> Round the world for ever and aye?

6   The class now chooses to be a part of that world, *eg*, seaweed, sea snakes, or sea beasts. Then the music and poem are repeated.
7   Members of the class are reminded of their slow motion movement exercises, practised in a previous lesson and each child places a chair, which represents a throne in the cavern and then he becomes the Sea King (music accompanies this).
8   In pairs—The Sea King and his wife (or where there are two boys they may prefer to be the Sea King and his son, just for this particular activity). First, they listen to the reasons for the return stated in the poem.

> ...O joy, O joy,
> For the humming street, and the child with its toy.
> For the priest, and the bell, and the holy well.
> For the wheel where I spun,
> And the blessed light of the sun.

The pair now improvise a conversation where one of them seeks to return to land. This is accompanied with a background of music. The scene ends where they part.
9   The Sea King, Margaret and a priest are cast. The rest of the class is divided into villagers, children and sea creatures.

The Play

The stage is the land, the hall the sea. Rostra are arranged near the shore as boats or rocks from which to fish. Also on the stage, a church is arranged and a stool is placed at one side on the apron stage, to represent Margaret's house.

There are times within the action, when one of the large groups is inactive. They are asked to remain relaxed, but as a still picture.

The fishermen and their wives are occupied at their various jobs ('Sea effects'). The church bells call them to prayer (Church music cross fades with *Daphnis and Chloe*). During the service the scene under the sea begins. The poem's description of the cavern (already mentioned), is spoken, plus a little more. This can be done chorally or individually by the children themselves with separate voices for the King and Queen. Additional lines which follow on after a pause...

> Once she sate with you and me,
> On a red gold throne in the heart of the sea,
> And the youngest sate on her knee.
> She combed its bright hair, and she tended it well,
> When down swung the sound of the far-off bell.
> She sighed, she looked up through the clear green sea.
> She said: 'I must go, for my kinsfolk pray
> In the little gray church on the shore to-day.
> 'Twill be Easter-time in the world—ah me!
> And I lose my poor soul, Merman, here with thee.'
> I said: 'Go up, dear heart, through the waves.
> Say thy prayer and come back to the kind sea-caves.'
> She smiled, she went up through the surf in the bay.
> Children dear, was it yesterday?

Margaret joins the people in the church. As the service ends they surround her asking for news. We hear the passage beginning 'O joy, O joy'. Then she breaks away and returns to her room (at the side, on the apron) and sits spinning. The villagers return to their homes.

Now the sea gets stormy (*Daphnis and Chloe* plus thunder effects) and the sea creatures are restless.

> She steals to the window, and looks at the sand;
> And over the sand at the sea;
> And her eyes are set in a stare;
> And anon there breaks a sigh,
> And anon there drops a tear,

From a sorrow-clouded eye,
And a heart sorrow-laden,
A long, long sigh
For the cold strange eyes of a little Mermaiden,
And the gleam of her golden hair.
The Sea King and the children come up to the shore and he
calls her....
    'Margaret!...Margaret!' (there is an echo.)
She shuts her window and continues spinning. The King and his
children return to the sea. (Music continues throughout.)
There dwells a loved one,
But cruel is she,
She left lonely forever
The kings of the sea.

Possible development
Members of the class may like to write a description of the
cavern when the King returns without Margaret, using the
same verse pattern as Mathew Arnold.
    Some children may like to express the poem in art or prose.
    A parallel scene where the mother is tempted to leave her
family and choose a different way of life, could be improvised
and used for discussion.

Drugged by Walter de la Mare (suitable for 13 to 15 year olds)
(The complete poems of Walter de la Mare 1969, Faber and
Faber.)
This is a poem which appeals to this age group because the
topic gains much publicity in the press and they are naturally
curious. Such a poem would fit into a project on *Drugs* or lead to
a profitable discussion.
Inert in his chair,
In a candle's guttering glow;
His bottle empty,
His fire sunk low;
With drug-sealed lids shut fast,
Unsated mouth ajar,
This darkened phantasm walks
Where nightmares are;

In a frenzy of life and light,
Crisscross—a menacing throng—
They gibe, they squeal at the stranger,
Jostling along,
Their faces cadaverous grey;
While on high from an attic stare
Horrors, in beauty apparelled,
Down the dark air.

A stream gurgles over its stones,
The chambers within are a-fire.
Stumble his shadowy feet
Through shine, through mire;
And the flames leap higher.
In vain yelps the wainscot mouse;
In vain beats the hour;
Vacant, his body must drowse
Until daybreak flower—
Staining these walls with its rose,
And the draughts of the morning shall stir
Cold on cold brow, cold hands,
And the wanderer
Back to flesh house must return.
Lone soul—in horror to see,
Than dream more meagre and awful,
Reality.

The Planning
1   The teacher reads the poem to the class.
2   White faced masks and percussion are needed. Members of
the class then experiment with the sounds and movement, wear-
ing the masks, as the teacher re-reads the passage where he
begins to dream.
    ' This darkened phantasm walks where nightmares are . . .'
The teacher should be aware of the need for contrasting speeds
within the lines of the poem.
3   They now choose someone to be the drug addict and arrange
themselves around him. He re-acts to their advance, trying
always to escape and although they never touch him, they are
always in his way. They now try to shape their movement, with

an artistic awareness of level, spacing and dramatic effect.

4   They try out the ending where the words suggest daylight and consciousness returning. The dream characters fade from his room.

5   The final combination of sound, music and movement.

The Ancient Mariner by Samuel Taylor Coleridge (suitable for 11 to 15 year olds)

The survival of the Hull trawlerman after the dreadful trawler losses of the Winter of 1967 and the return of many lone yachtsmen makes the story of the Ancient Mariner relevant to the young people of today. When do thoughts or hallucinations come to the man in solitude with death ever near? What must it be like to be in solitary confinement in a strange country, a prisoner by one's own unthinking actions?

Such discussion might open the lesson.

The Story

An ancient Mariner met three guests going to a wedding. He stopped one of them and started telling him his tale. The wedding guest is spellbound and finds himself compelled to listen. The Mariner tells how his ship was caught in a storm and driven towards the South Pole. When all seemed lost a great sea-bird called an Albatross came out of the fog and followed the ship. It appeared to be a good omen as the ship sailed through the icebergs. Then the Mariner told how he shot the bird with his crossbow and angered the rest of the crew. He continued to tell of his adventures and how the Albatross was revenged. One by one he had to witness the death of his friends, while he suffered many hallucinations. Eventually he felt the curse expiated and angelic spirits guided his ship towards his native land. As the ship started to sink, the Mariner was saved by the Pilot's boat. He begged a holy man to shrieve him and then ever since felt he must travel from land to land teaching, by his own example love and reverence to all things that God made and loved.

The Planning

1   The class sets the scene for a sixteenth century wedding. One of them is cast as the Mariner. This is an improvisation involving speech with music as a background. (Peter Warlock's

Capriol Suite or *Elizabethan Dances*.) Guests come and go being
introduced to the bride, groom and relations. The Mariner peers
through the doorway and eventually stops one of the guests
from entering.

2 After the wedding scene the first five verses are spoken over
the music. (The verses mentioned in the following notes are put
onto tape with a narrator or narrators, and different voices for
the other characters. Music links the improvisations with the
poem, while the previous 'living' picture freezes or is faded out
with a spot light. Sometimes the words accompany or precede
the action.)

3 The next section of the story takes place on the ship, with
a background of *Seagulls and Wash*. The sailors experience the
sudden arrival of a storm (wind and thunder effects), ice and
then fog. Eventually the Albatross comes to the ship and appears
to be a good omen because the fog lifts and a breeze gets up.
The Mariner shoots it with his crossbow and is accused by his
companions when the wind drops and they sail into a sea of
seaweed. This is improvised with speech.

4 Here the verses of the poem are taken up and spoken over
the action and music. (*The Painted Desert*, Grofé.)
from 'Down dropt the breeze...
to   ...the Albatross about my neck was hung.'
During this description, the girls in the group can create a movement sequence suggesting the slimy creatures and death fires,
dancing.

5 The death ship appears. The girls form the death ship which
moves towards the Mariner's boat, as the words are spoken.
(*Painted Desert* continued.)
from 'At first it seemed a little speck...
to   ...off shot the spectre bark.'

6 One by one they die, leaving only the ancient Mariner. He
sleeps
from 'O sleep it is a gentle thing...
to   ...it rained.'
He refreshes himself and to his amazement the dead men rise
and sail the ship. (Here masks can be used effectively and slow
motion movement. *Painted Desert* can be continued.)

7 The Mariner goes into a trance and the two polar spirits come
and discuss his plight. (Percussion or *Pavane pour une Infant*

Defunte, Ravel.)
from ' How long in that same fit I lay...
to ...the dead men stood together.'
8 They journey on and he sees his home land... (*Sea Interludes,*
Benjamin Britten or *Albatross,* Fleetwood Mac 57/3145.)
from ' A dream of joy. Is this indeed...
to ...like music on my heart.'
The angelic spirit leaves the dead bodies and they return to
corpses once more, but a seraph stands by each (the girls take the
parts of the seraphs).
9 The Pilot, his boy and the Hermit approach the boat.
from ' Why this is strange I trow...
to ...Push on, push on,' said the Hermit cheerily."
The boat sinks and they pull the Mariner into their boat. The
Pilot and his boy are afraid of him; the Mariner is delirious and
begs the hermit to shrieve him.
(*Sea Interludes,* Benjamin Britten.)
from ' O shrieve me, shrieve me, Holy man...
to ...to him my tale I teach.'
10 The scene returns to the wedding, the Mariner at last leaves
the guests and goes on his way (last two verses are spoken).

The wedding music should gradually fade during the last two
verses, so that the final verse is spoken in silence.

The amount of music used for the mime or to accompany the
tape is best decided with the group, as the process of piecing the
story, movement and music together is a most creative part of
that activity and one of which the older children are quite capable. Music has been suggested here, but most teachers would
prefer to find their own. It should be pieced together on tape so
that there are sections of sound which cross fade into each
other, providing that is the effect that is desired. Silence can be
equally dramatic in effect.

The staging needs to be flexible, so that the wedding scene
can have plenty of space and they can return to it at the end.
The movement of the ship is an illusion. The sinking can provide
an imaginative problem for the class. The story does divide its
cast into boys and girls, but there is plenty for everyone to do.

DRAMA AS A PRELUDE TO CREATIVE WRITING AND DISCUSSION

Creative Writing

Visual and musical stimuli are often used for creative writing, but some children find difficulty in projecting themselves into an imaginary situation and then writing about it. When the child actually acts out the experience with the musical stimulus, having also looked at photographs or paintings, having handled actual objects and had some preliminary help prior to the lesson in organising his ideas...then the writing will be alive and personal. The real experience is the perfect stimulus, but sometimes this is not possible and the simulated one has to take its place.

Take for example the topic *Fire*. The children have watched and smelt burning pieces of wood and paper and have written their immediate thoughts or descriptions. (See *English through Experience*, A. W. Rowe and Peter Emmens. Blond Educational Ltd.) Now this is extended. The class is studying in History 'The Great Fire of London' and here the two subjects could overlap and compliment each other. Illustrations are shown from the Jackdaw Series or any other source.

With enough space to move without distracting each other, they interpret their flight through London streets to the safety of the river, either as individuals or developing into groups where friends or families join together for the journey. Music such as *The Miraculous Mandarin* by Bartok accompanied by sound effects of fire and crowd noises could be used.

Some classes might have time to make a tape, themselves making the remarks and crowd effects.

The class could now sit in groups of about six and each in turn relate some part of their experience on that journey, when one stops the next person speaks, but relates his personal tale, not necessarily starting at the beginning and so on.

They now write, projecting themselves backwards in time.

The child will have heard and seen written on the board, words which described the burning of the wood and paper. Discussion following the movement will have produced words for mood and sensory experience.

How did you feel?
What did you hear?
What could you see?

What did you smell?

How did you run?

Did you have time to take anything with you?

Did you carry it or push it all the way?

Did you know the way?

Could you see?

Were you ever in actual danger?

Did you know how the fire started?

How fast did it spread?

Did you know where you wanted to go, did you just follow the crowd or did you wander about?

If preferred, similar discussion might precede the action. In an unstreamed class results may range from the simple but moving tale of a young child to the sophisticated writings of those who can assume another character in contact with many characters of the time.

Simple descriptions of Autumn, snow, animals or people; adventure stories of space, seaside holidays or old houses... can all benefit from either imaginative movement to music or the teacher's narration with a musical background.

Older children may prefer an overall theme, rather like a serial story. Take for example, an island, rather like the one in the Julian Slade musical *Free as Air*. A plane crashes in the sea and the passengers are rescued and stay on the island. The island has a newspaper and the class write articles for the paper. They decide on the events to take place each week and the journalist would have to interview some of the islanders before he could get his story. Here is the opportunity for drama. The interview, or the actual event whether comic or tragic, trivial or important.

Discussion

Discussion nearly always follows any drama done in the class-room, but the aim of the discussion will vary from lesson to lesson and from class to class. Discussion which aims at improving or understanding human behaviour is slightly different; and lengthy discussion, being the overall aid of the lesson, would take place mainly w.th fourteen or fifteen year olds. Here the drama need not necessarily be acted out by themselves; radio and television school broadcasts often provide excellent material. For

example, a television broadcast 'Danny misses School' looked at
this particular problem from many points of view, the mother's;
the man who wanted to marry her and the son's. Sometimes a
full length film can be used. If, however, such material is unobtainable at the time, the class members may themselves enjoy
setting up scenes which would illustrate the points needed for
the discussion, perhaps actually attempting script writing after
preliminary improvisations. There are also many scenes from
plays or novels which would provide the right stimulus. The
choice must inevitably rest with the teacher and the set plays
or novels for that particular school, would perhaps prove the best
material for that class, but here are a few examples of material
which would make interesting discussion with older children.

Z Cars scripts by Alan Plater (social and anti-social behaviour)

The Hand of Mary Constable by Paul Gallico (psychological
warfare)

Who's Afraid of Virginia Woolf? by Edward Albee (human
relationships)

Taste of Honey by Shelagh Delaney (human relationships)

The Insect Play by Karel Capek (a reflection of society)

Animal Farm by George Orwell (revolution)

1984 by George Orwell (future of society)

Out of the Silent Planet by C. S. Lewis (Science and the future)

The War of the Worlds by H. G. Wells (Science and the future)

The Visit by Friedrich Dürrenmatt (revenge and the acquisitive
society)

The Trojan Women by Jean-Paul Sartre (futility of war)

Worth a Hearing edited by Alfred Bradley. Blackie, (selection
of radio plays).

THE DRAMATIC INTERPRETATION OF PROSE

Many of the set literature books are ideal for dramatisation, while
others offer scripts of duologues or short scenes which can be
tried in pairs or small groups. These, ideally are tried in a hall
with the children working simultaneously, but otherwise in front
of the class by those able to memorise or read fluently with
expression.

C. S. Lewis's *The Lion, the Witch and the Wardrobe* is a great favourite for the younger age range and provides material for a wide range of dramatic activities. It is published by Collins, and can also be obtained in a Puffin paperback edition.

The Planning

1 In groups of four, the children explore a strange house, using speech. (Whether the class needs background music or not, depends upon its experience and absorption.)

2 Members of the class respond individually to the teacher's narration, the part of the story where Edmund's sister, Lucy, first gets into the wardrobe and finds herself in Nadia, explores and finds the strange creature who invites her to tea.

3 In pairs. The White Witch questions Edmund, tempts him with turkish delight and eventually lets him go. (Improvised or scripted directly from the text.)

4 In sixes—the scene at the Beaver's home during dinner, when Edmund flees to the White Witch. Scripted passage using the actual words of the book.

5 Edmund's journey to the house of the witch and his meeting with the statues. They respond individually to teacher's narration over sound effects or music such as *Fantasy after Dante* MFP 2024.

6 The transformation of Winter into Spring. Some teachers with an interest in dance drama, might like to use this story for a dance showing.

7 In fives. The rescuing of Edmund just when the witch is about to kill him.

8 A whole class activity. All the statues come to life when Aslan breathes on them and they are organised for battle.

9 A whole class activity. Fights are practised as an exercise first, if the class is inexperienced. The final fight, resulting in the death of the White Witch and the four are crowned rulers of Nadia. The class is divided into two sides.

10 In fours. The hunting of the white stag. (Here is a wonderful opportunity for the child to try out a different style of language.) While hunting for the white stag, they lose their way and arrive at the old lampost, now covered with a growth of plants. They find the entrance to the wardrobe and return.

Oliver Twist

Oliver Twist has been adapted for the open stage by Brian
Way and is ideal material for the middle years, as a production
or for stimulating interest in the novel. However some of the
dialogue in the novel itself is very suitable, for example, the
pick pocket scene with Fagin in the Den and the duologue
between Oliver and Noah Claypole in the Undertaker's shop.

The first scene is one where the child can easily identify himself with the weakling or the bully. Use of colloquial speech often
gives children confidence. The second scene demands good
improvisation from the gang of boys in Fagin's den; for the meal
of sausages around the fire and the game of 'pick pocket'. A
teacher who is interested in music, may like to include some of
the songs from the film *Oliver*. The social background of Fagin's
boys should be discussed and their personal attitudes towards
Fagin and each other. In this way the scene will become real and
they will be able to project themselves into the characters. Very
often this scene will give the teacher an opportunity to discuss
shop-lifting, without moralising. Help can then be given to those
who are tempted, so that they realise that light-handedness is
something they grow out of as they grow up and take their place
in society; that those who do not are disturbed in some way if
they have no real need to steal. With a child in the class actually
on probation for stealing, the teacher concerned would realise
just how far to continue such a discussion.

OLIVER TWIST
(Dialogue extracted from the novel by Charles Dickens)

NOAH CLAYPOLE   Open the door, will yer?
OLIVER   I will, directly, sir.
(Undoing the chain and turning the key)
NOAH CLAYPOLE   I suppose yer the new boy, ain't yer?
OLIVER   Yes, sir.
NOAH CLAYPOLE   How old are yer?
OLIVER   Ten, sir.
NOAH CLAYPOLE   Then I'll whop yer when I get in, you just

see if I don't, that's all, my work'us brat!
(*Begins to whistle*)

(*Oliver opens the door*)

OLIVER   I beg your pardon, sir; did you knock?
NOAH CLAYPOLE   I kicked.
OLIVER   Did you want a coffin, sir?
NOAH CLAYPOLE   Yer don't know who I am, I suppose, work'us?
OLIVER   No, sir.
NOAH CLAYPOLE   I'm Mister Noah Claypole, and you're under me. Take down the shutters, yer idle young ruffian!

DODGER   Now, then!
JACK DAWKINS   Plummy and slam!
DODGER   There's two on you. Who's the t'other one?
JACK DAWKINS   A new pal (*pulling Oliver forward*)
DODGER   Where did he come from?
JACK DAWKINS   Greenland. Is Fagin up stairs?
Yes, he's a sortin' the wipes. Up with you!

(*Dawkins and Oliver ascend the dark and broken stairs*)

JACK DAWKINS   This is him, Fagin, my friend Oliver Twist.
FAGIN   We are very glad to see you, Oliver, very.
Dodger, take off the sausages; and draw a tub near the fire for Oliver. Ah, you're a-staring at the pocket-handkerchiefs! eh, my dear! There are a good many of 'em ain't there? We've just looked 'em out, ready for the wash; that's all, Oliver; that's all. Ha ha! ha!
Well, I hope you've been at work this morning, my dears?
DODGER   Hard.
CHARLEY BATES   As nails.
FAGIN   Good boys, good boys! What have you got, Dodger?
DODGER   A couple of pocket-books.
FAGIN   Lined?
DODGER   Pretty well.
FAGIN   Not so heavy as they might be, but very neat and nicely made. Ingenious workman, ain't he, Oliver

OLIVER   Very, indeed, sir.

(Charley Bates laughs uproariously)

FAGIN   And what have you got, my dear?

CHARLEY BATES   Wipes *(produces four pocket-handkerchiefs)*

FAGIN   Well, they're very good ones, very. You haven't marked them well, though Charley; so the marks shall be picked out with a needle, and we'll teach Oliver how to do it. Shall us, Oliver, eh? Ha! ha! ha!

OLIVER   If you please, sir.

FAGIN   You'd like to be able to make pocket-handkerchiefs as easy as Charley Bates, wouldn't you, my dear?

OLIVER   Very much, indeed, if you'll teach me, sir.

CHARLEY BATES   He is so jolly green!

(The boys play the pick pocket game and Oliver watches. Then they make their farewells.)

FAGIN   There, my dear, that's a pleasant life, isn't it? They have gone out for the day.

OLIVER   Have they done work sir?

FAGIN   Yes, that is, unless they should unexpectedly come across any, when they are out; and they won't neglect it, if they do, my dear, depend upon it. Make 'em your models, my dear. Make 'em your models. Do everything they bid you, and take their advice in all matters—especially the Dodger's, my dear. He'll be a great man himself, and will make you one too, if you take pattern by him— Is my handkerchief hanging out of my pocket, my dear?

OLIVER   Yes, sir.

FAGIN   See if you can take it out, without my feeling it: as you saw them do, when we were at play this morning. Is it gone?

OLIVER   Here it is, sir.

FAGIN   You're a clever boy, my dear. I never saw a sharper lad. Here's a shilling for you. If you go on, in this way, you'll be the greatest man of the time. And now come here and I'll show you how to take the marks out of the handkerchiefs.

The Otterbury Incident by Cecil Day Lewis (Heinemann)
Many of the following scenes are excellent material for a drama
lesson, but the book makes an ideal plot for a play for middle
school children. The following notes do not follow the usual
pattern, but list the events as they could be rehearsed to develop
the whole into a play.

The best method of staging would be Avenue Arena, with the
audience sitting at the sides facing each other. The stage and
the other end of the hall could be used together with the centre
area. The characters are very well drawn, the children would
find qualities in the children in the book, which they possess
themselves. The scenery would be simple and calls upon the
imagination of the audience, relying on sound effects and mime
for some of the incidents. The market scene, where they raise
money for Nick, would enlist pupils who were good at physical
education, singing and dancing. The scenes are fairly short for
rehearsal purposes and the dialogue, apart from some crowd
improvisations, springs directly from the text.

Any drama work the children had done in the term which
involved imaginative music or mime; improvisation and charac-
terisation would enhance such a production and make rehearsals
a mere extension of the work.

Production notes
1   The classroom area becomes a river when the members of
the class (within the story) have been asked by the teacher to
remove the chairs and blackboard.
2   The impression of the dinghy moving is given by the boys
moving slowly forward.
3   Fights would need careful planning.
4   The church scene is portrayed on tape, until they reach the
tower.
5   Scene 13 needs to have pauses while the tension mounts and
everyone waits for Ted and Toppy to return. Adults pass, but
ignore the boys. The scenes inside Skinner's building must be
related by Toppy.
6   The lorry is imagined by sound and improvised reference.
The lorry is presumably parked just off the acting area, out of
sight.
7   The areas need to be lit as the action moves into them, by

spotlights which can be wired with long lengths of flex to *dip* switches on the floor at the sides of the stage, or to existing spot sockets in the front batten on the stage, which may not be in use.

Sound effects
Sounds of war to open the play.
Lorry.
Church music and echo of voices talking in hushed whispers, on tape.
Ambulance and police car sirens.
Trains.
Children playing.
Cheering audience.
Windows being broken.
Bell tolling.
Firing of rockets.
School assembly music to open and close the last scene.

Large vital properties
Toy tank with pedals.
Various rostra, steps, etc to indicate various areas.
Chairs.
Assembly table.
Blackboard.
Inflatable rubber dinghy.
Ladder.
Odd items of furniture in Rose's flat.
One stage flat, with a window in it.
Screens for the gates to Skinner's yard.

Scenario
1 Outside Skinner's yard. The mock battle.
2 Outside the school. The broken window. Headmaster and gang. Nick has to pay for the broken window.
3 The classroom.
4 The street. Skinner confronts Ted and George with a school cap found in his yard. Johnny Sharp covers up for them.
5 A meeting place. They decide on a plan to help Nick raise the money.
6 The town of Otterbury on Saturday morning—the market; general shoppers, etc. The boys and girls set about their plans

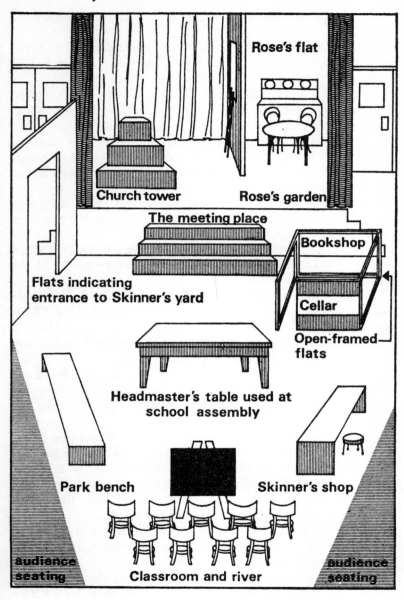

Suggested layout of acting areas

and raise £5 8s. 6d, which is put in a box, presented by the Prune.

7 Sunday. Rose's flat, above the shop—the money is discovered to be missing. Ted who had looked after the money is half accused of the theft and later there is a mock trial.

8 The street and Mr Sidebottom's shop. Later—Rose's garden and the street—the boys and Mr Sidebottom set to work as amateur detectives

9 The street. Their theories collapse, but they then discover a vital clue. Wart, Sharp's friend, gives the boys a half crown which they recognise as part of the missing money. They decide to question Prune.

10 The river side. Prune is questioned and finally confesses that Sharp and Wart gave him the box and suggested that they use it to collect the money.

11 Street and park—they track down Wart following Nick's arrow signs and frighten him into believing they have told the police.

12 The church and the tower. They follow him to the tower and are just about to make him sign a confession when Sharp appears and produces a knife. He and Wart lock the children in and they have to attract the attention of a passing errand boy in order to escape.

13 Outside Skinner's yard. The two gangs, armed, wait outside while Ted and Toppy enter. After a pause, Sharp, Wart and Skinner arrive in their lorry and go inside the yard shutting the gates behind them. Toppy manages to escape and relates their discovery of black market cigarettes and an old printing press, and tells the gang that Ted is in real danger. While one goes for the Police, the others attract Skinner's attention by throwing bricks at his windows. Then a real battle ensues, ending with Wart and Skinner tied up and Nick unconscious. Sharp has escaped. The Police and an ambulance arrive.

14 Street to river. Ted, Toppy and some others track Sharp to the river and fire rockets at his inflatable dinghy, overturning it. Sharp cannot swim. The Police arrive in time.

15 The school assembly. The Inspector and the Headmaster first deplore and then commend the boys behaviour. Nick is forgiven and the headmaster says the school will pay for the broken window.

Any of these scenes could be tried in the drama lesson without necessarily carrying the idea through to a production. If a hall was available, the large crowd scenes would be possible, but in the classroom situation, there are many chances to improvise in pairs or small groups. The mock trial could involve the whole class and the tape recording of the church scene, with the actors' voices also on the tape, could be an exercise in itself.

DOCUMENTARY ON WAR

The following is an example of a theme chosen and illustrated in a documentary style by a group of young people between 14 and 16 years of age. Some of the material was provided, but the group as a whole contributed to the shape of the documentary, the improvisations, the dance drama, the choice of visual and sound effects, the songs and the poems.

Sound effects Children playing cross fading with the tumult of war, which cross fades with a baby crying.

A BOY   Bradford Pioneer, Friday 27 July 1917.... I am making this statement as an act of wilful defiance of military authority, because I believe that war is being deliberately prolonged by those who have the power to end it.

I am a soldier, convinced that I am acting on behalf of soldiers. I believe that this war upon which I entered as a war of defence and liberation, has now become a war of aggression and conquest. I believe that the purposes for which I and my fellow-soldiers entered upon this war should have been so clearly stated as to have made it impossible to change them, and that, had this been done, the objects which actuated us would now be attainable by negotiation.

I have seen and endured the suffering of the troops, and I can no longer be a party to prolong these sufferings for ends which

I believe to be evil and unjust.

I am not protesting against the conduct of the war, but against the political errors and insincerities for which the fighting men are being sacrificed.

On behalf of those who are suffering now I make this protest against the deception which is being practised on them; also I believe that I may help to destroy the callous complacency with which the majority of those at home regard the continuance of agonies which they do not share, and which they have not sufficient imagination to realise. *Siegfried Sassoon*

A GIRL   O my brave brown companions, when your souls
         Flock silently away, and the eyeless dead
         Shame the wild beast of battle on the ridge,
         Death will stand grieving in that field of war
         Since your unvanquished hardihood is spent.
         And through some mooned Valhalla there will pass
         Battalions and battalions, scarred from hell;
         The unreturning army that was youth;
         The legions who have suffered and are dust.

A BOY   In November came the Armistice. I heard at the same time of the deaths of Frank Jones-Batman, who had gone back again just before the end, and Wilfrid Owen, who often used to send me poems from France. Armistice night hysteria did not touch our camp much, though some of the Canadians stationed there went down to Rhyl to celebrate in true overseas style. The news sent me out walking alone along the dyke above the marshes of Rhuddlan (an ancient battlefield, the Flodden of Wales) cursing and sobbing and thinking of the dead. Siegfried's famous poem celebrating the Armistice began:
         Everybody suddenly burst out singing,
         And I was filled with such delight
         As prisoned birds must find in freedom...
But 'everybody' did not include me.

Guitar and song   The Universal Soldier.

A GIRL   In 1939 war broke out again. Theatres, cinemas and

dance halls were closed. Newspapers were censored. Petrol and food were rationed. There was the threat of invasion.

A BOY Motorists leaving cars unattended are requested to remove the rotor arm from the distributor, thus immobilising the vehicle.

A GIRL Householders are advised to have buckets of sand and water in principal rooms, to keep the bath half full of water overnight and have a stirrup pump handy, and to stick strips of paper criss-cross on windows.

A GIRL All fireworks capable of being used for giving visible signals to the enemy are to be handed in. No person other than a servant of His Majesty is allowed to fly a kite or balloon.

A GIRL 13 June. The ringing of church bells was banned today. In future they will only be rung as a warning of an airborne attack.

Air raid siren followed by bombs

A BOY (*spoken during the air-raid*) It was like a shuttle service the way the German planes came up the Thames, the fires acting as a flare path. Often they were above the smoke. The search-lights bored into that black roof but couldn't penetrate it. They looked like long pillars supporting a black canopy. The shrapnel clicked on the road, and still the German bombers came....

A GIRL ...when this war is done
   The men's first instinct will be making homes,
   Meanwhile their foremost need is aerodromes,
   It being certain war has but begun,
   Peace would do wrong to our undying dead—
   The sons we offered might regret they died
   If we got nothing lasting in their stead.

Train effects (lines spoken when the train is still)

A BOY Today relatives waved farewell as their men were shipped to Calais to take part in the offensive against the Kaiser. Extra trains were laid on at Euston to take the conscripts to Dover. Churchill calls for still more volunteers....

A CHILD Mummy where's Daddy gone?

A WOMAN I thought the last one was the war to end all wars.

FARMER All these planes going t' put my cows right off milkin'.

GIRL   Mum, Bill's been called up, we're getting married on Saturday.
MOTHER   Don't worry son, and don't forget to write.

Bombs falling (lines spoken when sound is faded slightly)
A BOY   Cramped in that funnelled hole, they watched the dawn
          Open a jagged rim around; a yawn
          Of death's jaws, which had all but swallowed them
          Stuck in the bottom of his throat of phlegm.
          They were in one of many mouths of Hell
          Not seen of seers in visions; only felt
          As teeth of traps; when bones and the dead are smelt
          Under the mud where long ago they fell
          Mixed with the sour sharp odour of the shell.

The following scenes are played in a single spotlight in different areas. Bombs falling and explosion in the middle of the scene

TWO BOYS   *Improvised scene in the Trenches. An explosion announces a gas attack. One of them cannot reach his gas mask in time.*

TWO GIRLS   (Scene taken from *The Day of Glory* by H. E. Bates)
CATHERINE   In all the years I've known him I've never seen him behave as he did yesterday. Doesn't it occur to you why?
JULIA   It does occur to me, yes.
CATHERINE   Because of you. That's why.
JULIA   Not because of me.
CATHERINE   Yes. Because of you, I tell you! Why else should he have nearly killed me? Because he was driving with his arm round your neck! Why else should he ignore and humiliate me all day long? Because he was too busy struggling with a three weeks' infatuation with you.
JULIA   I tell you it was not because of that.
CATHERINE   Perhaps you'll also tell me why he tried to kill me?
JULIA   Yes, I'll tell you that. He almost killed you because he didn't see you.
CATHERINE   What nonsense. You saw me. Radwanski saw me. It was broad daylight. Why didn't he see me?

JULIA   He didn't see you because he wasn't there.

CATHERINE   Wasn't there? What are you talking about?

JULIA   Not entirely there.

CATHERINE   What in heaven's name do you mean? Not entirely there.

JULIA   Just that. Part of him was not there yesterday.

CATHERINE   Which to me is absolute nonsense. Raving nonsense. Do you suppose I haven't known him for three years without getting to know him as well as you have done in three weeks?

JULIA   There's such a thing as change in a man.

CATHERINE   Change! Oh! there's a change all right. If someone makes it.

JULIA   Someone? Isn't there something too? You seem to forget that men are doing things today that haven't been done in the world before. Flying at four hundred miles an hour. At forty thousand feet. Flying in burning aircraft for hours in darkness. Jumping into the sky. Killing each other five miles above the earth. Drifting for days in dinghies on the sea. And being alone —terribly and awfully alone—with a part of themselves they can never reveal. (*Passionately*) Do you suppose it doesn't alter the emotions they feel? Do you suppose it doesn't alter the men they are?

Blackout

TWO BOYS   (The scene is taken from *Journey's End by* R. C. Sheriff)

A Dugout.

STANHOPE   Hello; I thought you were asleep.

HIBBERT   I just wanted a word with you, Stanhope.

STANHOPE   Fire away.

HIBBERT   This neuralgia of mine. I'm awfully sorry. I'm afraid I can't stick it any longer....

STANHOPE   I know. It's rotten, isn't it? I've got it like hell....

HIBBERT   (*Taken aback*). You have?

STANHOPE   Had it for weeks.

HIBBERT   Well, I'm sorry, Stanhope. It's no good. I've tried damned hard; but I must go down.

STANHOPE   Go down—where?

HIBBERT   Why, go sick—go down the line. I must go into hospital and have some kind of treatment. (*There's a moment's silence*) I'll go right along now, I think....

STANHOPE You're going to stay here.

HIBBERT I'm going down to see the doctor. He'll send me to hospital when he understands.

STANHOPE I've seen the doctor. I saw him this morning. He won't send you to hospital, Hibbert; he'll send you back here. He promised me he would. (*Silence*) So you can save yourself a walk.

HIBBERT (*Fiercely*) What the hell....

STANHOPE Stop that.

HIBBERT I've a perfect right to go sick if I want to. The men can. Why can't an officer?

STANHOPE No man's sent down unless he's very ill. There's nothing wrong with you Hibbert. The German attack's on Thursday; almost for certain. You're going to stay here and see it out with the rest of us.

HIBBERT (*Hysterically*) I tell you, I can't...the pain's nearly sending me mad. I'm going. I've got my stuff packed. I'm going now...you can't stop me.

(*Stanhope gets out his revolver and by the time Hibbert returns, is looking at it thoughtfully*)....

HIBBERT Let's go by, Stanhope.

STANHOPE You're going to stay here and do your job.

HIBBERT Haven't I told you? I can't. Don't you understand? Let me get by.

STANHOPE Now look here, Hibbert. I've got a lot of work to do and no time to waste. Once and for all you're going to stay here and see it through with the rest of us.

HIBBERT I shall die of this pain if I don't go.

STANHOPE Better die of pain than be shot for deserting.

(*Hibbert breaks down*). *Blackout*

Marching sound effects

TWO BOYS AND A GIRL (*Improvised interrogation scene.*)

INTERROGATOR Bring her in! Sit down. What's your name?

PRISONER Marie Fallon.

INTERROGATOR Where do you live?

PRISONER 17 Rue de la Pays.

INTERROGATOR How many times have you helped them? (*No

reply) How many times? *(Grabs her hair)*
PRISONER   I haven't. *(He throws her back into the chair)*
INTERROGATOR   How many others live near you?
PRISONER   I don't know.
INTERROGATOR   You're lying. *(Grabs hair again and holds lit cigarette to her face.)* How many? How many? How many?
PRISONER   I tell you. I don't know.
INTERROGATOR   You're lying again....
PRISONER   I don't know, I don't know, I....
INTERROGATOR   You're lying....
PRISONER   No, no, no....*(She falls to the floor)*
Blackout.

Marching sound effects and machine guns
A GIRL   (A reading from part of *Anna Frank's Diary*)

A BOY Upon this battle depends the survival of Christian civilisation. Upon it depends our own British life and the long-continuity of our institutions and our Empire. The whole fury and might of the enemy must very soon be turned on us. Hitler knows that he will have to break us in this island or lose the war. If we can stand up to him, all Europe may be free and the life of the world may move forward into broad, sunlit uplands. But if we fail then the whole world, including the United States, including all that we have known and cared for, will sink into the abyss of a new Dark Age, made more sinister, and perhaps more protracted, by the light of perverted science. Let us therefore brace ourselves to our duties, and so bear ourselves that, if the British Empire and its Commonwealth last for a thousand years, men will still say, ' This was their finest hour '.

A GIRL   What passing-bells for these who die as cattle?
Only the monstrous anger of the guns.
Only the stuttering rifles' rapid rattle
Can patter out their hasty orisons.
No mockeries now for them; no prayers nor bells,
Nor any voice of mourning save the choirs,
The shrill, demented choirs of wailing shells;
And bugles calling for them from sad shires.

What candles may be held to speed them all?
Not in the hands of boys, but in their eyes
Shall shine the holy glimmer of goodbyes.
The pallor of girls' brows shall be their pall;
Their flowers the tenderness of patient minds,
And each slow dusk a drawing-down of blinds.

Guitar and song   Where Have all the Flowers Gone? (last 3 verses)

TWO GIRLS   *(Improvised scene on Hiroshima)*
INTERVIEWER   Can you tell our viewers exactly what happened on that day when the Americans dropped the first nuclear bomb?
WOMAN   I was in my house preparing a meal when I heard a plane fly over, then a few minutes later there was a blinding flash and when I came round I was lying in my garden. The house was in ruins. I got up and looked round me. Everything had been destroyed by the bomb. I don't know why but I began to walk, and as I walked I saw terrible fires on all sides of me and bleeding or mutilated people, just walking...walking...walking...

A BOY   ...*Yorkshire Times,* Friday 14 December 1947.
Lady Pemberton Roberts donates a thousand pounds for war memorial.
TWO GIRLS   *(Improvised scene. War Memorial)*
MAYORESS   Oh, Lady P. Roberts...do come in....
LADY P. R.   Lady Mayoress, how do you do? Now you know we must finally decide what sort of a war memorial we are going to have....
MAYORESS   Yes, well I....
LADY P. R.   I thought we could have a large granite slab set up, in the city park. I think it would be best there. Or would you prefer marble?
MAYORESS   Actually I....
LADY P. R.   Yes, I agree. Granite is more suitable. We shall have the names of the fallen on three sides, with Lord Pemberton Robert's at the top, of course....
MAYORESS   I was wondering....

LADY P. R.   With a laurel wreath and 'England expects' on the front.

MAYORESS   Well, I did wonder if the money might be more useful to set up a trust fund for the war widows.

LADY P. R.   Oh, my dear, we couldn't possibly do that...besides I've ordered the stone.

Slide showing starvation

A GIRL   'And ye shall hear of wars and rumours of wars
see that ye be not troubled; for all these things must come to pass, but the end is not yet.
For nation shall rise against nation, and kingdom against kingdom, and there shall be famines and pestilences and earthquakes in divers places.
All these are the beginning of sorrows.

A BOY   Britain accused of supplying arms to the Israelis.

ANOTHER   Economic sanctions on Rhodesia.

ANOTHER   Police fire on mob in Hong Hong.

ANOTHER   Nigerians bomb breakaway Biafra region.

ANOTHER   Twenty arrested in anti-Vietnam demonstrations.

ANOTHER   A group of young people carrying various banners were today removed from their 'sit down' protest outside No. 10 Downing Street.

SEVEN GIRLS AND ONE BOY   *(Improvised comedy scene. Ban the Bomb)*

Guitar   San Francisco played softly to accompany....

A GIRL   And he shall judge among the nations and shall rebuke many people and they shall beat their swords into ploughshares and their spears into pruning hooks, nation shall not lift up sword against nation, neither shall they learn war any more.

Guitar and song   The War drags on
(A dance drama is enacted to this. During the last verse masks are worn portraying the horrors of nuclear survival).

Slide of Skeleton and the last part of Vaughan Williams' Sixth Symphony.

A GIRL   Move him into the sun—
    Gently its touch awoke him once,
    At home, whispering of fields unsown.
    Always it woke him, even in France,
    Until this morning and this snow.
    If anything might rouse him now
    The kind old sun will know.
    Think how it wakes the seeds—
    Woke, once, the clays of a cold star.
    Are limbs, so dear,—achieved, are sides,
    Full nerved—still warm—too hard to stir?
    Was it for this the clay grew tall?
    —O what made fatuous sunbeams toil
    To break earth's sleep at all?

FURTHER REFERENCE
Living Expression Books 1 and 2 by John Hodgson and Ernest Richard, Ginn and Co.
Improvised Drama by Peter Chilver, Batsford.

Drama and Social Studies

HISTORY

The aim here is not only to impart facts which you hope will come back accurately in the dramatisation, but to give the child the experience of living at that particular time from as many viewpoints as possible. From the work that follows on the *Plague of London,* the class explores the themes of selfishness; superstition; ignorance; fear and dedication.

Work in a classroom is limiting in its scope for movement and treatment of the theme as a documentary, but the following activities are possible in a limited space.

Jackdaws

The *Jackdaw* series No. 2 (published by Jonathan Cape Ltd) gives a collection of detailed descriptions and documents which should be studied by the class and discussed with the teacher before attempting to dramatise the events. The absorption of the detail is very important to ensure the work is sincere. Where the child has not enough imagination to tackle the exercises below, the teacher will need to help the class by acting as leader of a particular group. For example, 'The Watchers' and then through appropriate question or statement he will enable them to project themselves with confidence and sincerity. If the class has little or no experience of drama, perhaps only the first exercise would be beneficial until they have gained more confidence. It might be necessary to have them seated at their desks and for the interviewer to walk among them. If exercise two and three were attempted, one group at a time might work, while the others watched.

Possible activities

1   The class divides into groups of about five and sits informally, if possible in a circle. Each member of the group chooses to be a certain person living at the time of the Plague and take it in turn to tell the other members of their group about themselves and how they were affected by the plague. If desired, the exercise could be repeated for a tape recording to be made, the teacher or a member of the class doing the interviewing. Either the anachronism of the tape recorder is glossed over or an imaginative reason is provided, such as a group of B.B.C. men arriving at the height of the plague, in their time machine from the year 2020. The exercise could be extended by the interviewees stating their ideas as to how the plague started and spread.

2   A list is compiled of the types of people who suffered or gained from the plague, such as:

The Rakers (who cleaned the streets of filth).

The Searchers (who were paid to search the body and state the cause of death).

The Watchers (who guarded the house which had been shut up and sealed).

The Sick and their families.

The Rich and their households.

The Priests.

The Grave diggers.

The Beggars.

The Apothecaries.

The Tavern keepers.

The Strolling Players.

The Mayor and his officials.

The Hangmen.

The Officers.

The Nurse keepers.

The Dog killers.

The Hackney Coach drivers.

A possible way of utilising this list is to ask members of the class to work in pairs, choosing to be one of the categories and to create a conversation which would take place between them expressing their opinions, their fears, their grumbles and their hopes.

Then, without making it a performance, but a sharing of ideas, each couple could repeat what they had done from where they were sitting. If the teacher could devise a way of indicating that their conversation was to fade into the distance while another couple began very softly and eventually took over, it would give an imaginative reason for more projection and also contain an element of 'theatre'.

3 Some classes may be used to getting into groups and working on their own plays. In this case, each group could work on different aspects and present them one after another as a documentary, either in front of the class or from the area of space where they created their scene. Some children feel more at ease if they can 'show' from the place they have used for rehearsal. Some scenes might be...

>A family discovering that one of them has the plague.
>An Apothecary's shop.
>The rich man deciding that he must leave London.
>The King's court.
>William Boghurst visiting St Giles.
>The Mayor and officials, drawing up the list of health regulations.

4 There are also opportunities for the class to work as a whole. The groups of people mentioned in exercise two, would automatically come into contact with each other as they go about their work. The tensions that would arise throughout the actual drama of trying to keep alive in that situation, would provide material for a class improvisation. This, in turn, would lead to discussion on the value at that time placed upon life, prayer and money.

Another whole class activity could take the form of a crowd scene. The Mayor's orders could be read or put up to be read and the crowd react to this. Similarly, the reaction of the poor could be compared to that of the rich, when a group of courtiers are forced, by necessity, to wander through an infected area.

LORD SHAFTESBURY AND THE CHILD WORKERS

The aim of dramatic activity with such a subject, is to enable the child to project itself more fully into the social conditions of the time; also to develop a concept of time and understand the development of social conditions in England from the nineteenth

century to the present day. The teacher may prefer to use literature to illustrate the lesson; for example with a few acted
excerpts from *The Water Babies* or *Oliver Twist*. On the other
hand a result of the following activities may be a documentary.
A teacher with an interest in music might produce an operetta
such as *The Little Sweep* from *Let's make an Opera* by Benjamin
Britten.

Suggested activities
Class conditions, both physical and social will determine the
extent of such creative work, but some of the items are possible
with little or no room to move, even if it does mean that eventually the groups have to come to the front to 'perform'. However items have been included which *do* need space in case the
school hall is available.
1 In pairs. A modern reporter questioning Lord Shaftesbury as
to why he bothered to take an interest in the working children.
2 Older children. In pairs or small groups. Lord Shaftesbury
approaches the Factory owners for better working hours and
conditions for the children.
3 Small groups. They create a family desperate for food and
shelter. They are in need of work and are willing to sell their
eldest child.
4 Large group work. The children create a nineteenth century
factory with some of them being the machines, while others are
the workers and overseers. Noise being an important item, some
suitable record or their own sound effects would be necessary.
5 Other short dramatic moments suitable for mime, improvisation or tape recording are:
    Lord Shaftesbury discovers a group of boys huddled near
    some chimneys.
    The Toshers, The Mudlarks and the Pure Finders describe
    their way of life.
    A young teacher tries to teach at a Ragged school with
    adults wanting to learn as well; some children falling asleep,
    others in need of clothing. All are hungry and she had
    hardly any equipment.
    An accident at the mines. Mime to music or an enquiry,
    where adults and children describe their job and the condi-
    tions at the time of the accident. Possible songs or scenes

from Alan Plater's *Close the Coalhouse Door* with songs by
Alec Glascow.
The death of a climbing boy. An enquiry.
Children giving evidence to the commission regarding their
deformities.
The trial of four children. Their charges and sentences.
6 Discussion of a television documentary such as *The Poor*
(Nottingham St Annes) which can be hired from the B.B.C.
7 Discussion about the future. 'What is the Welfare State?'
and ' Where do we go from here?'

THE ERA APPROACH   THE ELIZABETHANS

Many scripted plays have been written about this period, in
addition to the Elizabethan playwrights, and some classes would
benefit from reading some of the scenes in comparing supposed
fact to fiction.

Interviews with various people who might have lived at that
time would enable them to give the interviewer as much information as possible about their section. This method allows
the pupils to put forward both sides of an argument. For
example, Elizabeth and Mary Queen of Scots. Movement and
crowd improvisations are suggested by banquets, fashions,
prisons, discovery, rebellion, fairs, markets, dancing, bear baiting,
feasts and festivals.

The following sections provide rich material for class improvisations. At the end of term, six groups might choose a topic
from each section and then link the scenes together to give an
overall picture of Elizabethan life, rather like a documentary
linked with a little narrative, perhaps with passages taken from
poems or writings about this period.

Houses and Domestic Life
Architecture; halls and hovels; furniture and furnishings; food
and drink; gardens; banquets; smoking; clothes; fashions; family
life and education.

Exploration and Warfare
Ships; voyages of discovery; Drake and the ' Sea dogs'; trade;
Sir Walter Raleigh and Virginia; sailors and soldiers; weapons;
the Netherlands; war with Spain; the Armada.

Religion and Rebellion
The Church settlement; the Counter Reformation; Philip II;
Edmund Campion; Mary Queen of Scotts; John Knox; Puri-
tans; Huguenots; Henry IV and the Irish rebellion.

Town and Country
The London city companies; shops; the woollen industry;
apprentices; farming; enclosures; 'sturdy beggars'; the poor
law; roads; inns; merchants; fairs and markets.

Arts and Pastimes
Shakespeare and other writers; the Globe theatre; plays and
masques; musical instruments; madrigals; dancing; hawking
and other sports; bear gardens; cock fighting; feasts and festivals.

Government and Institutions
Queen Elizabeth; the Queen's favourites; the Royal household;
the court; the Royal progresses; the Queen's councillors; Parliament; Justices of the Peace and punishments.

GEOGRAPHY

The Fishing Industry project
Children who live at or near a sea port will be able to contribute
a great deal to such a project. Their relations would most probably be dock workers, trawler men or sea Captains. Their drama
would contain an element of reality, but for the children who do
not live near the sea and where a visit is not possible, the teacher
has to be able to convince them of the situation and be able to
describe it so vividly that they in turn, would be able to identify
and later dramatise any such events. That is why it is really
necessary for the teacher to have first or second hand experience
of visiting a fish dock, market or port if a great deal of drama
is to take place in the lesson. Books such as *Sea Harvest* (Uni-
lever) and *Let's go fishing* (Sea Information Service) provide a
great deal of information, but it is the personal touch which
makes a project 'live'. Walton Films sound film ' *To catch a
fish* ' is well worth hiring.

Suggested activities
1 A television advertisement. Groups arrange one on 'Fish'.
2 As a follow up to this. In pairs or threes—two housewives,

with a very poor knowledge of the names of fish, ask the fish-monger to help them choose.

3 Weather Forecasts. An actual broadcast is used on tape for an example, and then the children create one for themselves such as:

(*a*) Winds moderate. Sunny. Temperature 22° Centigrade. A group then enact the scene on a trawler in these conditions.

(*b*) Gale force winds. Snow. Temperature Minus 10° Centigrade.

A similar scene on the trawler with desperate efforts to fish and yet keep alive.

4 News or newspaper reports, with interviews with the relations of the trawlermen about accidents, safety precautions, working conditions, and their lonely lives. (Tape recorder could be used here.)

5 Small groups. The local inshore fishermen. The family scene which portrays his reliance on luck and the weather *or* a friendly discussion over a drink or meal between either trawlermen and inshore fishermen (or between their wives) on the differences of their trade.

6 The Salmon catchers are interviewed by a reporter.

7 A whole class activity. The fish markets. Fish are auctioned at an early morning market.

8 In pairs and then perhaps sharing with the class. Two employees try to persuade a friend to come and work with them. They describe the work and conditions.

9 All these activities could be linked together to form a documentary which could be shown to other classes at the end of the project. Suitable music might be 'Singing the Fishing', Charles Parker. *Argo* Radio Ballad, R.G.502.

RELIGION

The Parable of the Good Samaritan

'And, Behold, a certain lawyer stood up, and tempted him, saying, Master, what shall I do to inherit eternal life?

He said unto him, What is written in the law? How readest thou?

And he answering said, Thou shalt love the Lord thy God with all thy heart, and with all thy soul, and with all thy strength, and with all thy mind; and thy neighbour as thyself.

And he said unto him, Thou hast answered right; this do, and thou shalt live.

But, he, willing to justify himself, said unto Jesus, And who is my neighbour?

And Jesus answering said, A certain man went down from Jerusalem to Jericho and fell among thieves, which stripped him of his raiment, and wounded him, and departed, leaving him half dead. And by chance there came down a certain priest that way; and when he saw him he passed by on the other side. And likewise a Levite, when he was at the place, came and looked on him, and passed by on the other side. But a certain Samaritan, as he journeyed, came where he was, and when he saw him, he had compassion on him, and went to him, and bound up his wounds, pouring in oil and wine, and set him on his own beast, and brought him to an inn, and took care of him. And on the morrow when he departed, he took out two pence, and gave them to the host, and said unto him, Take care of him; and whatsoever thou spendest more, when I come again, I will repay thee.

Which now of these three, thinkest thou, was neighbour unto him that fell among the thieves?

And he said, He that showed mercy on him. Then Jesus said unto him, Go and do thou likewise.'

This parable is particularly relevant in a world where there is so much suffering, fighting and starvation that we are apt to sit back and let other people get on with it. When young people do demonstrate in a passive way they are regarded as stupid, time wasters or lay-abouts. When they demonstrate with barricades and violence they are looked upon as outlaws.

Suggested activities
1   There is the obvious miming of the incident with musical background or improvising the scene in small groups.
2   The modern parallel of the street gang fight or injured policeman, can be arranged and then discussed.
3   There should be an opportunity for the class to think and contribute ideas for a modern parallel which is perhaps more subtle than activity number two.
4   The responsibility for the unknown person, because he is a fellow human being...

Lying to achieve one's own ends.
Sending someone on a ' wild goose chase '.
Seeing a child playing in danger and ignoring it.
Spreading gossip which has no foundation.
5   For those who feel deeply about war and peace, the man who
fell among thieves symbolises Peace, and the Good Samaritan,
Hope. A dance drama could be created around this idea.
6   Up to date events could be used for improvisation, whether
local or national, whether headline or back page news.

The Parable of the Talents
' The Rector has given £125 towards the Parish Church Hall
Appeal (which includes improved central heating to the church),
to be used in the form of Talents. It is hoped that 125 people
will accept £1 each, and by their efforts and ingenuity ' make it
work' so that it will increase (like the Gospel story St Matthew
25, verses 14-30). Already many have intimated their willingness
to participate in this scheme. If you are able to share in it too,
please complete the form of receipt opposite and bring it with
you to a Communion Service at one of the three churches on
Sunday 16 March, when it will be exchanged for £1 cash (or
after that date, on application to the Rector personally). This
'Talent' should be returned on 19 July, which is being marked
as a Gift Day. This gives exactly 125 days for you to make the
£1 increase, in whatever ways you decide. Please make the
scheme known among your non-church-going friends, as this
will have the advantage of advertising it as widely as possible.'

Here is the drama of real life expressing the Parable of the
Talents. It provides as much of a challenge today as it did then.

' For the Kingdom of Heaven is as a man travelling into a far
country, who called his own servants, and delivered until them
his goods. And unto one he gave five talents, to another two, and
to another one; to every man according to his several ability; and
straightway took his journey.
Then he that had received the five talents went and traded
with the same and made them another five talents.
And likewise he that had received two, he also gained another
two. But he that had received one went and digged in the earth,
and hid his Lord's money.

After a long time the Lord of those servants cometh, and reckoneth with them.

And so he that had received five talents came and brought other five talents saying, Lord, thou deliveredst me five talents; behold I have gained beside them five talents more.

His Lord said unto him, Well done, thou good and faithful servant; thou hast been faithful over a few things, I will make thee ruler over many things; enter thou into the joy of the Lord.

He also that had received two talents came and said, Lord, thou deliveredst unto me two talents; behold I have gained two other talents beside them.

His Lord said unto him, Well done, good and faithful servant; thou hast been faithful over a few things, I will make thee ruler over many things; enter thou into the joy of the Lord.

Then he which received the one talent came and said, Lord I knew thee that thou art an hard man, reaping where thou has not sown and gathering where thou hast not strawed.

And I was afraid, and went and hid thy talent in the earth; Lo, there, thou hast that is thine.

His Lord answered and said unto him, Thou wicked and slothful servant, thou knowest that I reap where I sowed not, and gather where I have not strawed, Thou oughtest to have put they money to the exchangers, and then at my coming I should have received my own usury.

Take therefore the talent from him and give it unto him that hath ten talents.

For unto everyone that hath shall be given and he shall have abundance but from him that hath not shall be taken away, even that which he hath. And cast ye the unprofitable servant into outer darkness. There shall be weeping and gnashing of teeth.'

Suggested activities

1   Discussion to consider God's gifts and the good use we make of them. Personal gifts such as musical, practical, academic or social talents or gifts such as...

    the company of friends and relations
    the beauty of the earth
    the friendship of animals
    the discovery of scientific power and invention
    the balance of nature

the gift of communication.

2 From these items and any others suggested by the class, scenes can be divided which show good and bad use of such gifts.

eg The family situation where overcrowded conditions set up tension which completely obliterate any friendship there might have been. Some incident brings a little peace into the family and there is a ray of hope and love which lasts perhaps for only a short time.

A motorway is planned to cut through some of the most beautiful countryside. There is a public meeting where members of the public air their opinions.

A child's picture book version of the farm is contrasted with the battery hens, the calfs kept for veal, the ritual slaughter ...in a documentary; with poems from childhood; songs from Peter Terson's play *The Ballad of the Artificial Mash;* excerpts from newspaper cuttings; characters from Parliament, farms; religious institutions; etc.

The morality of germ warfare and the effects of a nuclear explosion. Suitable material for a dance drama, debate, improvisation in pairs or small groups.

The effect of insecticides on plants and birds, sea life and cattle. New born babies and their resistance to antibiotics.

The strike because of lack of communication between the workers and the management.

The girl who lost her first job, because she communicated an expression of insolence to her employer and was not able to explain that he had been mistaken.

The broken marriage because neither can really say what they want or feel.

There are many poems, novels and plays which embrace these or other ideas and the teacher may be able to include some of them, so extending the literary knowledge of the group.

FURTHER REFERENCE
The Defiant Ones by Brian Peachment, Pergamon Religious Educational Press.

Drama and remedial classes

In most remedial classes there is a large proportion of disturbed children with a sense of failure, either academically or in personal relationships. These are children who are in most need of the therapy which educational drama can provide, but they disagree violently with each other, swinging in mood from one day to the next. They possess little self-control and find difficulty in concentrating for any length of time. Re-acting in an immature way, they respond to excessive freedom like infants let out into the playground after a long rainy day. They tend to be over aggressive or meekly unresponsive, preferring lethargic daydreaming. Dissatisfied with their roles in society or uncertain of what their role should be, they secretly long to succeed, to please and to create.

With a teacher they know well and can trust they can overcome these difficulties and begin to achieve some success in many subjects, but drama offers activities which not only absorb a great deal of their physical energy, but replaces it with a feeling of peace, which few of these children ever have a chance of experiencing. Music therapy is used in many schools for the handicapped and educationally sub-normal. Music also acts as a control when used within the drama lesson. When the control is built into the activity and the group are accustomed to listening and responding to the music, the teacher's task is much easier.

Although they would probably feel less strange in their classroom, the closeness of their companions makes absorption difficult and they do need the space of a hall to 'play'. They will enjoy arranging the rostra and building a spaceship or a den. This will take them a long time with much arguing and indecision, but they can be helped over this by carefully given instructions or the teacher arranging the hall beforehand so that if there are to be four groups, each group has a certain number of rostra, chairs etc, which they can use and have to take from their own corner only. Repetition of simple rules needed in the lesson will help them feel that they have achieved success in organisation and co-operation. Very often a little praise given just before it is deserved encourages the group to believe in their own ability and so next time achieve it for themselves.

Movement exercises which seem like games make a very good start. The ability to stop with the music should be given as a challenge, not as an order.

Older pupils... Pop instrumental music such as *Stars fell upon Stockton* by The Shadows, makes an ideal backing for games such as 'Follow the leader'. Here the leader goes anywhere in the hall (within the limits set out in the rules), changing the style of movement, legs or arms as he goes. Similarly, the movement can be changed when the leader is changed. They should be encouraged to explore patterns on the floor *eg* taking the line in an S shape to differing rhythms of the music.

Musical statues... Again using music which is familiar to them, they take a mimed activity such as dancing in a discotheque; or cleaning the car; road sweeping; chasing a balloon...and stop as the music stops.

Fast and slow motion movement... Here you would need a twin turntable record player or taped music with a varied amount of fast and slow music. They take a mimed activity such as a ball game in twos and follow the music as it FADES from one to the other. THEY FIND IT VERY DIFFICULT TO MOVE IN SLOW MOTION AND SO IT PROVIDES QUITE A CHALLENGE.

Some girls who cannot dance to Pop music find it embarrassing to try in front of their friends and they would prefer to act out a mannequin parade to music. This gives opportunity for creative writing, describing the clothes, and the best readers a chance to be the commentators.

*Younger pupils...*The movement session can lead into a story and the progression follows that of the average child, but the

disturbed child progresses at a much slower pace and may never
achieve a stage where they can successfully build a good story for
themselves without help. However, they can achieve success in
the early stages and will enjoy making up their own stories. The
interpretation as a group might be more successful if the earlier
methods of teacher's narration or breaking down into activities
were used to express them.

Dr Who music immediately works from the known to the unknown. They may want to mimic the stories they have already
watched, but they will be equally as enthusiastic to create their
own and involve themselves rather than the television characters.
As a movement exercise they can explore the planet accompanied
by the music, but when it stops they are under a strange power
and find they cannot move. This is another version of musical
statues, but they are involving their imaginations and in the
story that follows the teacher has an imaginative control.

Sample Story
Either in pairs or on their own, they leave their space ship to
explore the planet. They find that they can breathe and that they
walk much slower than usual. They discover some strange rocks.
They see a beam of light and discover that they cannot go
through it It is hard like glass. They go round it and see a
strange creature; they wrestle with it and eventually escape.
They realise that when the sounds of the planet stop, they cannot
move. After the fight with the creature, they decide to return
to the space ship, but are overcome by a strange gas and find
they can go no further. They lose consciousness.

   This story is deliberately short and narrated by the teacher
over the music. Occasionally the music is stopped to practise the
control, but then the story is taken up again without losing their
absorption. If they are working in pairs, they will be greatly
tempted to fight each other and therefore they may all like to be
the creature before the story begins. They may be able to describe it. If such a fight does develop it may distract the rest of the
class and develop into a feud between two boys instead of
creature and explorer. The ending of the story is there as a
de-climax (a calming down effect). Now if it is possible to change
the music to something like *Little Princess* by The Shadows,
without there being any break, they will be able to relax for a

few moments while the teacher goes very quietly among them, saying something like this: 'I'm coming to see if you're really unconscious:; your arms will feel like lead, your head will be floppy if I touch it: you still hear me but you will feel far away....' Then as the music fades they are asked to get up very slowly. It is then you may hear a remark such as:

'Wasn't that good, Miss. I've never felt like that before....'

For a very short period there has been a suspension of belief. Older children will want to act out stories which reflect their home life and the characters which surround them. Girls especially would 'play out' home situations for weeks on end, while boys prefer to 'play' at violence, including torture and sadistic primitive behaviour. Whether the latter is 'playing out' or 'practice' must be judged by the teacher concerned, but it could act as a basis for extending them into a story concerning violence and the important discussion which would follow. For example, a prisoner of war camp; an assassination; famine; or two leaders struggling for power. In these stories the teacher can act as leader taking the group into a scene by participating himself and the children cast themselves as the story enfolds. Every so often they stop to decide Why? Where? and When?

Why is violence necessary?

Where will they make the escape tunnel?

When will be the right time to escape?

The 'domestic' scenes of the girls provide opportunity for development into scenes which depict correct home or social behaviour.

eg, Bringing the boy-friend home for the first time.

The elder sister decides to leave home.

Their parents have said they must be home by 10 pm. They arrive late.

Younger children may also act out domestic and violent scenes, but mostly it will be adventures seen on television or caricatures of home and school. The child who always gets an attentive audience when he's 'funny' will lead his group into scenes where he shines as comedian. Again, these are all starting points to develop their own powers of creativity and to help them discover their own role in school or home. The rejected child is often a problem, when no one will partner them and the class openly states, ' She smells ' or, ' I'm not sitting next to 'im! '

While forgetting themselves, they also tend to forget the real
life roles they have given each other and discover that co-operation is possible. They find that such a child is necessary for their
story and that perhaps he has more ability than they realised....
'He was quite good, Miss, wasn't he?'

It is better for them to work with friends or those they can
work with, rather than forcing a grouping which could only
bring about more arguments. Some children may want to work
together but always cause trouble. Then it is up to the teacher's
discretion. Given some responsibility, the pair may work usefully
and their leadership qualities, if any, channelled to positive effect.

When these children have acted out their immediate needs
they can be stimulated imaginatively by 'props', simple costumes
such as lengths of material or headdresses, music, pictures or
film. However, their ideas still need guiding into a framework
so that they feel they know where they are going and so succeed.

Where the teacher enjoys working with music, the class will
also respond to it and enjoy simple mimes to music and later
be able to develop their movement into simple dance drama. The
following is an example of a simple mime which can be taught to
the class. Being taught a set mime can sometimes give confidence
to children who otherwise would never attempt it. It should not
be an end, but a means to a beginning.

The Park Bench—Music—The *Harry Lime* theme played at slow
speed.

Lady with a baby in a pram.
City gentleman in bowler hat with brief case and rolled umbrella.
Tramp with a banana.

The lady pushes the pram towards the bench, sits on it, coos
to the baby, takes out a magazine or powders her nose. *On the
next phrase of the music* The gentleman comes to the bench,
tips his hat to the lady, sits, undoes his brief case, takes out his
sandwiches, places his hat at his side and eats. *On the next phrase
of the music* The tramp enters, sees that his favourite bench
is occupied and wanders around wondering what to do. He
examines the contents of the litter basket and then sits on the
end of the bench next to the gentleman. The gentleman retrieves
his hat just in time. The tramp thinks of a good idea. *On the*

next phrase of the music He begins to scratch in time with the music. Eventually the gentleman also begins to scratch, gets his things together and moves away. The tramp moves up and starts again. The lady also begins to scratch and she eventually moves. On the last few bars, the tramp triumphant puts his feet up, covers his face with his cap and sleeps.

FURTHER REFERENCE

Experience and Spontaneity by Peter Slade, Longmans.

Scope, Schools Council Publications Co.

Play, Drama and thought by Richard Courtney, Cassell.

Teaching English to Immigrants by June Derrick, Education Today, Language Teaching Series, Longmans.

Look, listen and learn by L. G. Alexander, Longmans.

Drama with immigrants

Many classes in big cities have a fair proportion of immigrants and the normal drama which takes place in the school is of special benefit to their language development. The narrated story is a form of comprehension; imaginative movement followed by description, enables them to practise the past tense and playing at fighting helps them to understand that this is possible without actually hurting each other. Some Pakistani children find it difficult to understand that many children who play roughly in the playground do so for fun. Although any child placed in a similar situation, would experience great frustration and imagine insult or injustice.

Some teachers have small groups of immigrants for short periods of time every day. The progress achieved in learning English varies from child to child. Those who know very little, need confidence to speak outside the normal drill. Taking the simple structures which they have already learned, the teacher can construct a scene which they are likely to experience, *eg*, in the playground, or the shop.

The playground
CHILD 1   Can I play with you?
CHILD 2   No, you can't.
CHILD 1   Please, let me play with you.
CHILD 2   Oh, all right. Catch.
CHILD 1   Here you are...catch.
CHILD 3   That's my ball!
CHILD 2   No, it isn't, it's Ali's ball.
CHILD 3   No, it's mine.
CHILD 2   It's his.

CHILD 1   It's mine.
CHILD 2   It's his ball. Give it back to him.
TEACHER   What's the matter?
CHILD 3 and CHILD 1   It's my ball.
CHILD 2   No, it's Ali's.
TEACHER   Whose ball is that? (*points to another similar ball*)
CHILD 3   Oh it's mine. It's just the same. Sorry.

In the shop
SHOPKEEPER   Hello, what do you want?
CHILD   Can I have a packet of sweets, a tin of soup and a jar of jam, please?
SHOPKEEPER   Which sweets do you want? These....or those.
CHILD   Those, up there. The red ones. Thank you.
SHOPKEEPER   What kind of soup, do you want?
CHILD   Tomato please.
SHOPKEEPER   This one or that one?
CHILD   It doesn't matter. The cheapest.
SHOPKEEPER   What else was it you asked for?
CHILD   Jam.
SHOPKEEPER   Oh yes. Which flavour? Strawberry, apricot, raspberry?
CHILD   Strawberry please.
SHOPKEEPER   Right. That will be six and two.
CHILD   Here's ten shillings.
SHOPKEEPER   And here's your change. Can you carry them?
CHILD   Yes thank you. Goodbye.
SHOPKEEPER   Goodbye.

Here the teacher has in fact given them a script, but it is taught by repetition so that the children learn the correct inflections and emphasis.

There comes a time in their language development when they are capable of creating a little for themselves within a framework of similar dialogue. For example, group story telling with the teacher leading....

'The King woke up suddenly, he heard a... Then he went to the door and called... He turned round and saw...so he ran back to the bedroom and....'

Similarly in an acted scene... 'The King has been sent for because some people have been found outside the Palace gate.

They suspect they are spies. They are brought before the King
and accused. They defend themselves....'

The beginning dialogue is given but those children who are
capable of expanding the dialogue for themselves have the freedom to do so. Others less confident are helped by their friends or
the teacher and the repetition of the scene helps them to
memorise the structures involved.

Although the scenes need to be repeated, this should not be
overdone. It would be more beneficial to create a new story
around similar structures.

Glove puppets made with junk materials can be used where
there is not enough space to act, or as an introduction to such
work, when the children are very excitable. The shy child will
hide behind the puppet, but make it talk and this can be a big
step towards finally taking on for himself the responsibility of
talking in another language. Leaflets on the making of junk
puppets can be obtained from The Educational Puppetry Asso-
ciation, 23a Southampton Place, London W.C.1.

If slides are available of popular stories such as *Robin Hood*
and *Snow White,* a tape can be made to accompany them. In a
later lesson the group will feel confident enough to re-enact the
story using a mixture of their own words and those used on the
tape. This could then be followed with written work. ' Look and
Learn Slides ' from Montrate Ltd, Sandwich, Kent have a comprehensive list.

Where children have difficulty in remembering the correct
order of words, physical movement helps them, *eg,* ' No, he isn't
here today ' usually becomes...'Today, he no here.' Simple linking gestures remedies this in a very short time. Words of action
and mood are similarly learned.

A PERSONAL CONCLUSION

The response of the immigrant child to dramatic activity em-
phasises the need of the average English speaking child. It is
easy to forget that many children suffer a handicap in language.
They have plenty of opportunity to talk among themselves, but
lack conversational activities on a progressive level. They are
often allowed to make up their own plays (therapeutically valuable), but lack the knowledge of structure and vocabulary to

produce scenes which will extend their abilities. The teacher may well presume the children understand the concepts of the words he uses and then be very surprised to discover in the yearly tests, that 25 per cent of the class have failed to use accurately words such as *plural, opposite* or *describe.*

This failure in language and understanding, and therefore in academic achievement often gives rise to frustration and despair. This in turn can create in the child a dislike of self, school and those in positions of authority. In primitive tribes great care was taken to ensure that the language was successfully passed on from one generation to the other. The grandmothers would gather children around them and tell them stories, occasionally omitting parts so that the children could suggest appropriate words. We can no longer rely on the family. There is such little time in many households, for conversation or bedtime stories. Television and comics are the substitutes.

The immigrant's case is easy to diagnose and special help is usually given until most of the hurdles have been passed and the child 'chats' easily in the local dialect. Many English speaking children, from poor cultural environments are fortunate if they progress beyond this stage. Large classes and the inability of some teachers to recognise the individuals needs, hinders their language development. We are so used to our own language that we take it for granted we are communicating. When you are confronted with those who do not understand English, you suddenly realise both for the immigrant and the deprived English child, just how much repetition is needed; how much drama is relevant to their lives; how much oral work and story telling; and most important of all—how much they need to experience success.

Every child has an ability to express himself in some way, whatever his intelligence quotient. If he is not given the opportunity, he may soon be convinced he has nothing to say.

...And as they express they achieve an understanding and hence a mastery of what their thoughts and feelings are expressing, and come to know of themselves in the process....

Education Survey No. 2 DRAMA (HMSO.)
Department of Education and Science

SECTION TEN

Record list

Denotes records which give a reasonable quantity of contrasting material

Adagio for Organ and Strings, Albinoni, TVS 34135. Very beautiful organ music suitable for background to improvisation or linking scenes in a production.

Aida, Grand march, Verdi, LXT 6139.

L'Après-midi d'un Faune, Debussy, FUA 10111. Gentle and flowing.

L'Arlésienne Suite, Bizet, XLP 20044. Varied, some good gentle bits.

Bach *Chorales,* CEP 686. Useful church music. *Sleepers Awake* is suitable to accompany mime.

Billy the Kid, Copland, ABL 3357. Gun fight and fun of the fair.

The Birds, Respighi, MMA 11053.

Capriol Suite, Peter Warlock, 7 EP 7063. Medieval music, suitable for controlled work in pairs or groups.

Carnival of the Animals, Saint-Saëns, *Divertissement,* Ibert MFP 2041. All of the *Carnival* is useful, especially *Aquarium,* for under the sea scenes; Ibert's *Finale* suggests anything from riotous drunks to washing an elephant. The *Cortège* suggests a humorous procession. It occasionally breaks into a discordant wedding march.

Concerto for guitar and orchestra, Segovia, 33 OX 1020.

Concert Percussion, John Cage, Time s/8000. Available from Discurio, 9 Shepherd Street, London W.1. Splendid clashing sword march Side A. No. 3. March which could be played at 45 for this effect.

Dance Symphony, Copland, RB 6641. Suitable for dance drama.

Danse Macabre, Saint Saëns, ACL 37.

Daphnis and Chloë, Ravel, ACL 53. Ideal record for under the sea music, both lyrical and dramatic. Choir in background occasionally.

The Music of Edgar Varese, Columbia MS 6146. This record is only obtainable from America, but can be ordered from Discurio, 9 Shepherd Street, London W.1, but may take three months to obtain. It contains *Ionisation; Density 21.5; Integrales; Octandre; Hyperprisme* and *Poème Electronique.* The latter suggests, many things, but to give you an idea, it is reminiscent of the after effects of atomic war, vague background war noises from time to time, discordant church bells and beat music...the other bands are useful for anything suggesting space, fear or weird surroundings.

*Electronic Movements, Disseveldt, 430 736 PE. Delightful rhythms suggesting another planet. *Drifting* is especially suitable for exploring a planet.

Enigma Variations, Elgar, ACL 55. Varied, solemn, stately, strong and calm.

Façade Suite, Walton, VIC 1168.

Fall River Legend, Columbia ML 4616 (U.S.A.)

Fantasy after Dante/Romeo and Juliet Overture, MFP 2024. Good storm sequence, suggests the elements. A good fight scene with clashing swords in the *Overture.*

La Fille Mal Gardée, Harold Lanchbery, LXT 5682. Very useful record, especially the *Clog dance,* the *Storm* and *Lise and the Ribbon.* Could be used for many ideas. Music is both light and lyrical, yet also very dramatic.

*Firebird Suite/Rites of Spring, Stravinsky, Philips GEL 5612. Suggests strange, weird surroundings and a chase. Some good climaxes.

The Fireworks, Stravinsky. Suast 50479.

Four Sea Interludes, Britten, ACL 162. *Storm* is especially dramatic. It has a quiet passage in the middle and builds up a climax at the end, very good for dance drama as a whole... witches or a storm at sea.

German String music of the seventeenth century, OL 50175.

Giselle, Adam, G.L. 5776.

Grand Canyon Suite/Mississippi Suite, Grofe, CAP P.8347. Very descriptive pieces. *Painted Desert* suggests heat and loneliness. *Mississippi Suite* contains passage with melody of old-fashioned musical box.

Harry Janos Suite, Kodaly, MFP 20 42. *The Fairy Tale Begins,* magic chord, suitable for entry of Pied Piper; *Viennese Musical clock,* gay, quick march with bells; *Song,* very sad, suitable background for improvisation; *Battle and Defeat of Napoleon,* march interrupted by loud crashes, musical shrieks and sudden stops. It suggests Ogre or interrupted journey; *Entrance of the Emperor and his Court,* gay crowd scenes, or processions, slightly humorous.

Job, Vaughan Williams, LXT 2937.

Legend of the Jivaro, Yma Sumac, CAP T 770. War cry, nerve shattering sound and eerie background.

The Love of Three Oranges, Prokofiev, MPF 2047. Tchaikovsky's *Nutcracker Suite* is on the other side. Dramatic music, menacing at times. A quiet passage at the end.

Love for Three Oranges, Prokofiev, ALP 818.

Midsummer Marriage. 4 Ritual dances, Tippett, ZDA 19-20. Also *Second Symphony.*

Miraculous Mandarin/Music for Strings, Percussion and Celeste, Bartok, SXL 6111. Evil, weird and builds to a climax with abrupt stops. Suggests urgency and chase. *Miraculous Mandarin* similar, but more discordant.

Missa Criola, Philips B.L. 7684. Suggests journey of slaves towards the promised land.

Mother Goose Suite, Ravel, XLP 30067. H.M.V. Concert Classics Series. *The Fairy Garden* provides music for a procession of wonder and humility, with a climax at the end.

Music for the Flute, William Kincaid, ML 4339, U.S.A. Columbia. Haunting music. Shepherd's pipes or early morning scenes.

Music for Trumpet and Orchestra, Purcell/Vivaldi, ALC R56.

New World Symphony, Dvorak, FDY 2009. Evolution and regal at times.

Night on a Bare Mountain, Mussorgsky, FDY 2045. Excellent for fights, with an imaginative control of bells followed by a very sad melody.

On Hearing the First Cuckoo in Spring, Delius, 7ER 5198. Quiet meditative mood.

Les Patineurs, Mayerbeer/*Le Cid,* Massenet, ACL 62.

Pavane pour une Infante Défunte, Ravel, BM 2119. Slow, sad
'ody.

̃ynt, Grieg, CEP 5521. Dramatic building of slow climax

in the *Hall of the Mountain King;* other bands are quiet and beautiful.

Pictures at an Exhibition, Mussorgsky, Parlophone PLP 106. *The Gnome,* very dramatic, quick movements with sudden stops, then flowing. Sounds evil and distorted. *The Old Castle,* rather sad and medieval. *Ballet of the Unhatched Chicks,* title speaks for itself, could be used for puppet movement. *Two Polish Jews,* two contrasting themes which occur separately at first and later together. *The Market Place at Limoges,* good market background for improvisation. A good substitute for *Trisch Trasch Polka* if played at speed. *The Hut on Fowl's Legs,* menacing and dramatic attack, with middle passage suggesting grovelling distortion. *The Great Gate of Kiev,* ending is excellent for procession or an endings suggesting grandeur, religious festival, a climax or well-being.

*Planet Suite, Holst, MFP 2014. *Mars,* warlike and threatening, storm. *Venus,* quiet flowing melody, suitable for meditation, dreams. A good substitute for *On Hearing the First Cuckoo. Mercury,* staccato, quick moving, rippling, tinkling. *Jupiter,* light, gay, yet majestic, suggests royal courts. *Saturn,* at first sounds like eerie footsteps. Could be used for exploring a planet. Climax of discordant bells. *Uranus,* dramatic opening, magician type music. Rather like the *Sorcerer's Apprentice. Neptune,* very quiet, under the sea, rippling music.

Rites of the Pagan, Elizabeth Waldo. C.N.P. VA 8009.

Ritual Fire Dance, de Falla, SX 6187.

Russian orchestral compositions, FUC 10069.

Sabre Dance, Khachaturian, FAP 1 8438.

El Salón Mexico, Copland, MMA 11005. Exciting and fast with some strong beats.

The Seasons, Glazunov/*The Wise Virgins,* Bach arr. Walton. ACL 218.

The Seasons, Vivaldi, ACL 91. Very descriptive music suitable for background to spoken verse.

Scythian Suite Op. 20, Prokofiev, DO 13495. Ivanov. U.S.S.R.S.S.

Sinfonietta for Orchestra, Janaček, GGC 4004. Includes triumphal procession, suitable for a Roman festival.

The Sorcerer's Apprentice, Dukas, XLP 30092.

Sylvia, Délibes, MFP 2022. *Pizzicato* is suitable for anything from a caretaker dusting a museum to catching a mouse in an attic.

Symphonic Poems, Smetana, LPV 451.

Symphony No. 5, Sibelius. Decca BR 3068.

Symphony No. 6 in E. Minor, Vaughan Williams, ACL 289. Both are very dramatic and offer possibilities for linking scenes in production or for dance drama. Long pianissimo passage at the end of the symphony.

The Three-Cornered Hat, de Falla, ACL 182. Varied with one good strong section.

Trisch Trasch Polka, SCD 2111. Good for a chase if played faster, or for Victorian mime.

Trumpet Fanfares, Decca F.9281.

Vivaldi-Bach, *Concerto No. 2 in A minor*/Franck, *Trois Chorales,* ACL 246. Organ music dramatic and serene.

Walk to Paradise Garden, Delius, ACL 144. Stately and beautiful.

The Wasps, Aristophanic Suite, Vaughan Williams. March past of the *Kitchen Utensils,* ACL 247-8.

Albatross, Fleetwood Mac, 57-3145

American piano music, XID 5209.

L'Amitié, Françoise Hardy, VRE 5015. Sung in French. Suitable for slow, ritualistic movement.

Back to back, Duke Ellington, CLP 1316.

Basic Indian Album, RCA Victor, E.89. U.S.A. Ceremonials, chants, dances and lullabies of tribes.

Bye, Bye Blues, Polydor HiFi 84 046. Magic land, freedom of movement and wonder.

Cast your Fate to the Wind, Sounds Orchestral, 7N 35206. Good and evil theme, strong or weak, etc.

Chicago, The Living Legends, RLP 398.

Concert by the Sea, Leroy Anderson, BBE 12184. As above.

Continental Jazz, GGL 0054.

Dr Who theme, F.11837. *Batman* theme, MAL 626.

Duke Ellington, B.B.E. 12273, Philips.

Duke Ellington, SOC 1031 and CBS 52421.

Earl Hines, SL 10116.

Eighteenth-century Rock, Parlophone 4594. Interchanges genuine

eighteenth-century music with a pop version.
Flamenco, CM 2128.
Gershwin Rhapsody in Blue, GGL 0099.
Harry Lime Theme, F. 9235. Slower tempo than above.
*Hushabye, GGL 0075. This includes *Whistling Rufus* which is gay and lively. *Hushabye* is suitable for slow motion movement.
I was Kaiser Bill's Batman, DM 112. As above.
International Folk Lore, M.981 Concert Hall.
Jazz, Shearing, Acker Bilk, Becket and Reinhardt.
*Journey into Melody, Robert Farnon, GGL 0291. This contains *Jumping Bean; Portrait of a Flirt;* and *Poodle Parade.* Suitable for any lively activity.
Jungle Drums, Decca. DL 5426 U.S.A. Weird, strange sounds.
Lawrence of Arabia, PXE 300. As above.
*Little Princess, The Shadows, DB 7416. Slow motion or sun bathing.
Lonely Bull, Herb Alpert, SL 10027.
Los Indios Tabajaras, Maria Elena, RCA 1365. U.S.A. Suitable for slow motion movement.
Mexican Corn, Herb Alpert. E.M.I. SE 1037.
*Mr Malcolm goes to Town, CEP 5502. Fast moving, suitable for imaginary ball games etc.
*Moving Percussion and Electronic Sound Pictures (A Listen, Move and Dance record), CLP 3531. Side two is especially useful and cover notes are most explicit. On one record you have space, monsters, machines, conversation in jabber talk, underwater effects and many other bands suitable for creative movement, pair or group work.
Music for Dancing and Mime, Barbara Lander, DCL 281/282/283. (Available with free 8-page booklet from Discourses Ltd, 10a High Street, Tunbridge Wells, Kent.)
Music for Silent Films, PRE 668, humorous.
Nola/Little Rock Getaway, EAP 1 20145. As above.
Parade of the Russ Conway hits, SEG 8175. As above.
Shish Kebab, Ted Heath, DFE 6432. Persian Market.
*Sounds Orchestral, Piccadilly. NPL. 38014.
South of the Border, Herb Alpert. NPL 28051.
Spanish Flea, 7N 25335.
Stars Fell on Stockton, The Shadows, SEG 8171. Humorous.
Stories in Movement, Rachel Percival.

Persephone, 7 EG 8976. *Beowulf,* 7 EG 8977. *Pantalone's Panto-mime,* 7 EG 8981. Available from EMI Records (Education Dept) 20 Manchester Square, London W.1.
Stranger on the Shore, Acker Bilk, SEG 8156. Slow and lyrical.
Swinging Shepherd Blues, DFE 6487. As above.
A Walk in the Black Forest, MF 861. As above.
West Side Story, Bernstein, BBL 7277. Suitable for dance drama.
World Accordion Test Pieces, Marcosignori, ACL 1137. Drama-tic or humorous. *Danza Orientale* makes ideal background for a magician's act.
The World of Light Music, CLP 1836.
Zorba's Dance, DRS 54001.

Drama Workshop, The Seasons, RESR 7.
Movement, Music and Mime, RESR 5.
Obtainable from Brian Keyser, BBC, TV Enterprises, Villiers House, Haven Green, London, W5.